40 days

to reflection and peace

thoughts for busy people and ethical leaders

Art Sathoff

1st WORLD
PUBLISHING

40 DAYS

to reflection and peace: thoughts for busy people and ethical leaders

Art Sathoff

Copyright © Art Sathoff 2014

Published by 1st World Publishing
P.O. Box 2211, Fairfield, Iowa 52556
tel: 641-209-5000 • fax: 866-440-5234
web: www.1stworldpublishing.com

First Edition

LCCN: 2014902455
ISBN: 978-1-59540-918-8

Acknowledgements

I would first like to acknowledge my wife and sons, who believed I had a book in me and encouraged me to write it. I thank and acknowledge my reason for living, God, Who has so richly blessed me and enabled me to grow in Him. I thank and acknowledge all of the great people I have worked with through the years as a teacher, coach, and school administrator. I owe a huge debt of gratitude to all of the great thinkers and leaders I have read and listened to through the years. I am grateful for the spiritual guidance and teaching of Pastor Frosty Van Voorst, our minister of over 20 years, and of Pastor Jim Wakelin, my mentor in the licensed ministry program. Finally, I am thankful for the ministers' retreat, which was the impetus for this book.

Foreword

This book surprised me. In a good way.

I have known Art Sathoff for years, but only in his role as a school district administrator. I knew nothing of his active life as a husband, father, and pastor. I was unaware of his past as a teacher, coach, and star student athlete – an inductee into the Iowa Basketball Hall of Fame. It takes a unique and powerful set of character traits and leadership skills to build such an impressive resume. And in *40 DAYS to Reflection and Peace* these qualities leap off every page. In forty discrete essays, Art draws upon his experiences to help his readers maximize their strengths and overcome their weaknesses. He presents any aspiring leader the opportunity to better understand what it takes to build a great organization, and, more importantly, how to succeed as a human being. His reflections caught me off guard and quietly changed my life.

There is nothing formal or overbearing about his approach. Art weaves his stories and the lessons they contain using natural, unassuming prose. The words flow out as comfortably as though he were sitting next to you in a car on a long ride home. That said, he is not shy. He is emphatic in stressing the need to get the "big things" right. He speaks of the value of family and work. He writes with conviction of the importance and blessings of faith. There are moments when his deep and abiding belief in God lights up the page. He makes the case that personal and professional success are advanced by adherence to the laws of nature and nature's God. But I never detected hubris or a hint of self-importance. He never claims ownership of the ideas or recommendations he presents.

Art has read widely. He is thoughtful. He listens carefully. In the course of a few pages, he can reference the Bible, Shakespeare, Thoreau, John Wooden, Clark Griswold, and Radar O'Reilly. And the subtle transformative power of this book springs from his ability to synthesize the thoughts of these and many others and offer his conclusions in a way that encourages us to think more deeply about our journey and what it takes to succeed.

I am sure that Art did not set out to change the world when he wrote this book. It is clear that he believes that each of us is possessed of certain greatness. He has a profound commitment to provide authentic leadership: to help those around him fulfill their aspirations. Perhaps he was led by his natural impulse to inspire the better angels of our nature. Whatever his intentions, his words helped me be a better man.

Jamie Vollmer

Author of *Schools Cannot Do It Alone*

Day 1:

What do you want on your tombstone?

Do you remember the Tombstone pizza commercial that ended with the tagline, "What do you want on your tombstone?" I thought that was a clever ad because it tapped into universal human needs and questions. We have a need to make some kind of a mark on the world. A lot of people call that "leaving a legacy." In moments of doubt, we have the questions, too: "Will anyone miss me when I'm gone? Have I made any difference in the world?"

I'm an old English teacher, and I used to have students write their obituaries. I'm not even sure I would give that assignment today in our litigious society full of troubled teens, but it would do students well to stop and think about how they want to be remembered. If I had done a better job of that when I was a teenager, I would have been a kinder person, I'm sure. I do believe our God is a God of second chances (and third and fourth chances, etc.), but there are natural consequences of sin. We hurt others and ourselves, and we live in ways that we regret later.

If we could follow one of Stephen Covey's *7 Habits of Highly Effective People,* "Begin with the end in mind," living the epitaph that we want on our tombstone, embodying the obituary we want in the paper, how much happier would we be and how much surer would we be that we are leaving a positive legacy?

There are many stories and symbols that illustrate the impact we have on others: the ripple effect of a stone tossed in the water, a butterfly flapping its wings on one continent and impacting the weather on another one, a boy named Kyle saved from suicide when someone helped him pick up his books, the hitch hiker who helped the wealthy businessman accept Christ the same day he died—Google them and enjoy. More importantly, live like you know your life makes a difference in the lives of others; we impact everyone we meet one way or another. Find out, like the boy who pounded a nail into a fence every time that he lashed out in anger, that each nail, all 37 in his case, leaves a scar, even when it is pulled out of the fence.

Most of us won't have the odd experience of reading our own obituary in the paper like Alfred Nobel did. When Nobel's brother died, a careless journalist eulogized the "King of Dynamite" instead. Nobel re-wrote his story to be remembered for the Nobel Peace Prize, not as a merchant of death. We write the story of our lives, too. Actually, we're just ghostwriters because God is the real brains of the operation. That's the approach I'm taking with this book. I have felt called to write before and even started once before, but now I'm just being a mouthpiece for God. I'm going to write what I feel like He is leading me to write for the next 40 days, and I hope someone might find some benefit in it.

Let me leave you with this today: if you haven't thought about this before, think about it now and write it down— What do you want on your tombstone? What will your epitaph be? Here's mine: "He served God, loved his family, and worked hard." Faith, family, and work: those are my "big rocks," but that's for another day.

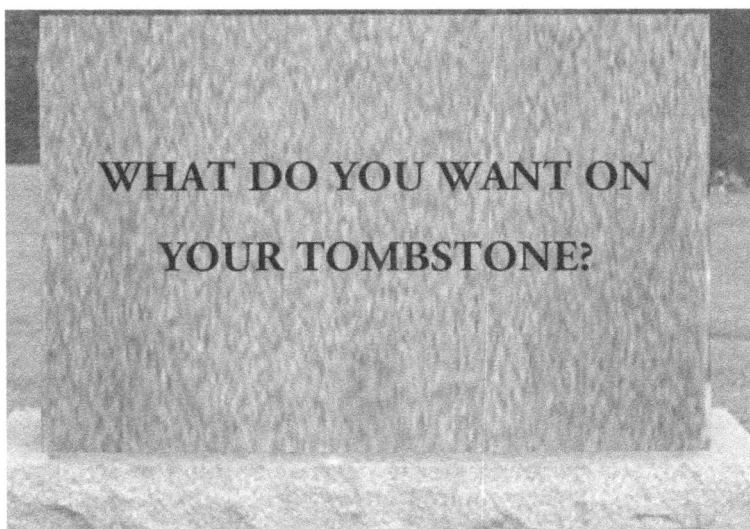

Day 2:

The Big Rocks

"Be still, my soul, for God is on your side," was my centering thought as we entered silent meditation for half an hour this morning. We were about thirteen hours into "The Great Silence," which I am not sure I took full advantage of. While I didn't talk, I certainly was not monastic as I texted back and forth with Cindy, followed the Bulls' progress in a disappointing road loss to the Pacers on my iPad, and played "Dice with Buddies" on my smart phone with my cousin Lance. I consider myself a fairly reflective person, but I have to say that all of this sitting silently and meditating and praying for extended periods of time has been different. To some extent, I don't feel like inward is where my focus should be, at least exclusively inward. A few years ago the Christian Church of the Upper Midwest had "Inward, Outward, Upward" as its assembly theme. That balance captures what the life of a Christian should be pretty well, I think.

I do believe focus is especially important. I've heard, "You hit what you aim at," and I think that's true. I believe people tend to rise to the level of expectation. I know, as a coach, that what's important is what gets emphasized. I know, as a competitor, that it matters when you're keeping score. I have always been a person who seeks mental models, or paradigms, to help make sense of the world and guide my life. The Bible, of course, is the ultimate guidebook, but I like John Wooden's *Pyramid of Success*, I find truth in John Maxwell's *5 Levels of Leadership* and other books, and I see wisdom in Stephen Covey's *7 Habits of Highly Effective People*. I learn from a good story, too. I strive for the right growing conditions. I want to be the good soil in the Parable of the Sower (See Matthew 13).

One extremely meaningful story, which has been told and retold in different forms, is the story of the Big Rocks. Once I heard this and really figured out what my big rocks were, probably in my early thirties, my life totally changed. As Roy Disney said, "Once you know what you believe, there are no hard decisions." Let me share the story of the Big Rocks with you here:

"Big Rocks" Time Management Demonstration

One day an expert in time management was speaking to a group of business students and, to drive home a point, used an illustration those students will never forget. As he stood in front of the group of high-powered overachievers, he said, "Okay, time for a quiz." Then he pulled out a one-gallon wide-mouthed Mason jar and set it on the table in front of him. Then he produced about a dozen fist-sized rocks and carefully placed them, one at a time, into the jar. When the jar was filled to the top and no more rocks would fit inside, he asked, "Is this jar full?"

Everyone in the class said, "Yes."

Then he said, "Really?" He reached under the table and pulled out a bucket of gravel. Then he dumped some gravel in and shook the jar, causing pieces of gravel to work themselves down into the space between the big rocks. Then he asked the group once more, "Is the jar full?" By this time the class was on to him.

"Probably not," one of them answered.

"Good!" he replied. He reached under the table and brought out a bucket of sand. He started dumping the sand in the jar, and it went into all of the spaces left between the rocks and the gravel. Once more he asked the question, "Is this jar full?"

"No!" the class shouted.

Once again he said, "Good." Then he grabbed a pitcher of water and began to pour it in until the jar was filled to the brim. Then he looked at the class and asked, "What is the point of this illustration?"

One eager beaver raised his hand and said, "The point is, no matter how full your schedule is, if you try really hard you can always fit some more things in it!"

"No," the speaker replied, "That's not the point. The truth this illustration teaches us is: If you don't put the big rocks in first, you'll never get them in at all." (Cheryl Drangsteveit)

My big rocks are faith, family, and work. These things get my focus, my attention, my time, my energy, and my heart. There is a prioritization there, too, which I will explain. I understand that this is an exclusive list that doesn't contain certain things that would show up in others' rock collections. That's the beauty of picking your own rocks.

Let me start with why work is #3 for me. Work is incredibly important. I believe we were created to work. "You reap what you sow," Galatians 6:7 tells us. God set the example: He labored; He created. Then He rested. Paul told the early Christians in Thessalonica that if they wanted to eat, they should work (2 Thessalonians 3:6-13). I put my heart, my time, and my energy into my work. I want to be the best school superintendent and pastor I can be. I believe our work is our creation, and we ought to autograph it with excellence. I find joy in my work. I embrace both the responsibility of school operations and the opportunity to serve people and help them grow. Volunteering for the school as an unpaid coach allows me another opportunity to help young people grow and succeed. It also allows me to placate my competitive gene a little. Having the opportunity to work as a pastor is a great honor, too. I get to be God's messenger on a weekly, daily, even hourly basis. I am a student of God's Word, and I am a communicator of His redemptive plan. I could help prepare a heart so that it is fertile ground for the work of the Spirit! That's exciting work, helping to prepare a soul harvest for God. I also get to share in some of the most joyful and heart-wrenching moments in people's lives: officiating at weddings and funerals. In those cases I ask God to give me the words people need to hear. A common prayer I offer to God is, "Lord, please speak to me and through me."

As significant, invigorating, and fulfilling as work is for me, do you suppose there are times when work can't give me everything I need? Do you suppose that even an eternal optimist could get discouraged, fatigued, and weighed down? Ask my wife. This is why family is #2 for me. I am blessed and defined by my incredible wife and awesome sons. I could never be as good of a person, "the man I am," without them. I don't say that out of ego, in a "look at me" way. I say that out of contentment because I am so incredibly blessed to have the wife and two sons I have. Without them and without the important purpose of being the best husband and father I can be, I shudder to think where I would be. I remember my young adult life before Cindy and the boys, and that is not how I want to live.

Family was important to me growing up. The importance of family has been reinforced for me as my parents and other loved ones have passed away. One good thing about Facebook and Smart phones is that I have re-connected with some extended family in recent years, too. I know that my family is there for me when I face challenges in work and life.

There's something that comes before even family, though, and that's faith. There are family crises and things the family can't handle itself. Where is the family to turn in these times of challenge? I hope they have a relationship with their Creator and a family of believers to turn to. Jesus said it Himself: "Who is my mother, and who are my brothers?" [49] Pointing to his disciples, he said, "Here are my mother and my brothers. [50] For whoever does the will of my Father in heaven is my brother and sister and mother" (Matthew 12:48-50).

I struggled for a long time with Jesus' pronouncement, "If anyone comes to me and does not hate father and mother, wife and children, brothers and sisters – yes, even their own life – such a person cannot be my disciple." (Luke 14:26) and with His seemingly callous comment, "Let the dead bury their own dead" (Matthew 8:22, Luke 9:60). He is telling us what our first rock must be: The Rock. "On Christ the solid rock I stand. All other ground is sinking sand!" ("My Hope is Built on Nothing Less" by Edward Mote, 1797-1874)

Yesterday I asked you to write your epitaph. I bet you couldn't do that very easily if you don't know your big rocks. Do you remember my epitaph? "He served God, loved his family, and worked hard." There you have my big rocks, in order: faith, family, work. I invite you to identify your big rocks right now. If you have never articulated them and never written them down, they are not as firmly in place as they need to be. There's nothing magical about the number three (EXCEPT the triune God—Father, Son, and Holy Spirit), but I question the human capacity to really focus on more than three things at once. I invite you right now to identify your big rocks. In schoolwork we talk about "grain size." These rocks are boulders. They are the BIG things in your life, not the pebbles or the countless grains of sand. Good luck!

"WHAT ARE YOUR BIG ROCKS?"

Day 3:

Beyond Ability

Ability is great; don't get me wrong. Ability is a God-given gift or talent that has been developed through stewardship and hard work. Ability is not a quick fix or a pill to be prescribed, which is why I hate *Abilify*, which I see advertised often, even though I don't really know what it does. Ability will only take a person so far, though. As Hall of Fame Coach John Wooden said, "Ability may get you to the top, but it takes character to keep you there." With that in mind, I would like to offer a few important "ilities" beyond ability.

Accountability—The extent to which we are accountable to God and to those we love will largely determine our satisfaction with life. The Bible says obedience is the first sign of love. (See John 14:15, John 14:23, 1 John 5:3, 2 John 1:6) I know that striving to live a disciplined life has positively impacted me tremendously.

Reliability—Woody Allen once said, "Ninety percent of success is showing up." Reliability is related to accountability. Others depend on us, and we depend on others. In my 2013-2014 administrative team handbook, the first expectation I communicated to my admin team was, "Take care of your stuff." Pretty impressive, huh? Sometimes simple is the best. Be reliable. Take care of your stuff.

Responsibility—You should be sensing a theme here. Responsibility fits right in with accountability and reliability. I think of responsibility more as a role I should seek than something I have to do. Being willing to step up and take responsibility is leadership. In his book *Sometimes You Win, Sometimes You Learn* John Maxwell states, "Responsibility is the most important ability that a person can possess. Nothing happens to advance our potential until we step up and say, 'I am responsible.' If you don't take responsibility, you give up control of your life" (53). Owning failures and committing to addressing them and improving is powerful. Doing so takes some <u>humility</u> (a bonus "ility" for you). Humility does not mean a lack of confidence. On the contrary, humble leaders can have great confidence because their trust is in the Lord, not themselves. The first thing to take responsibility for is our sins. We are sinners. We are imperfect, but we serve a Perfect God, Who loves us. Say the prayer of the tax collector: "God, have mercy on me, a sinner." (Luke 18:13) Own your sins. That's responsibility.

Hillbillity—As the proud father of 1.5 redneck sons (Older son Jordan likes to shop and is a project manager, so he gets .5 in honor of his love of guns, hunting, fishing, and bowling league.), I appreciate hillbillity. I have lived my adult life in Northwest Missouri (briefly) and Southeast Iowa, so I have come to love country music, the quiet life, redneck ingenuity, and being able to laugh at myself. Maybe this "ility" isn't as earth shaking as some others, but it belongs on the list. It reminds us to have a little fun and not take ourselves too seriously. Oh, the other redneck son, who gets the full 1.0, is our camo-wearing son Trey, who studies Ag business at Graceland University when he isn't hunting or fishing. His coach texted me, "He cracks me up. He showed up to practice with bloody boots and hands today." Trey had gutted a deer just before practice. Thankfully, Coach understands. Trey has his guns at Coach's house and his venison in Coach's freezer.

Nobility—I think I could play this word game all day, but I have responsibility and accountability to get to my day job, so I close today with nobility. You know, don't you, that we are a "royal priesthood," God's chosen people? (1 Peter 2:9) We are adopted heirs in the family of God, "joint heirs with Christ" (Romans 8:17). Each one of us is nobility, and while I don't intend to look down my nose at hillbilly, I do remember that I am special because God has consecrated me, or set me apart, to glorify Him. We are called to be Holy, or like God. We are to strive to become more Christ-like each day. That is a huge responsibility and we will have accountability on the Day of Judgment. We have been given much, and "To whom much is given, much is expected" (Luke 12:48). Have a great day! God loves you!

Day 4:
The Oracle and the Bard

The ancient Greek city of Delphi had a highly regarded oracle to which many people came to hear their fortune or get guidance. My Great Uncle Art got to visit the site of the oracle with a bunch of Simpson College students late in his life, and he saw the three small holes in the rock, where the legs of a high three-legged stool were inserted. At the center of the three small holes was a larger opening in the rock, where noxious fumes once rolled up out of the earth. A priestess, really still a girl, would sit on the high stool and become loopy as she inhaled the gasses. As she babbled away, the priest stood at a safe distance and "interpreted" the oracle for the visitor.

Some things never change. People still look for guidance and meaning in the strangest places. I will say one thing: the visitors did get good advice from the inscription over the entry to the oracle. In fact, they might have been better off if they had just read the inscription, turned around and headed for home, and thought about it. The inscription read, "Know Thyself."

I believe knowing thyself comes before personal growth, which comes before helping others. A random thought just occurred: even in the airplane safety spiel they tell you to put your own mask on first before trying to assist others. Is that selfish or practical and necessary? Knowing thyself is really being honest with oneself, and then a person can move on to loving oneself and improving oneself.

I know myself. I have an addictive, or hyper-competitive, personality. If I were a single non-Christian, I'd probably live near a casino, enjoy the night life too much, or go thrill seeking. I would treat the world as my playground and be deeply unhappy. Since I'm an incurable smart aleck, I would alienate people instead of helping them. I might do some good by accident because God has gifted me with some leadership skills. I might be successful at work though eventually I would have a big crack up or ruin my health.

This is not the way I live because I know myself, and I have the Big Rocks I wrote about earlier: faith, family, and work (Day 2). I have lived like the prodigal son to some degree (See Luke 15:11-32), and I'm never going back. I urge you, if you know someone in the grips of what the world sells us as fun/happiness, try to guide him/her to a relationship with Jesus.

So, there you have the oracle, but what about the Bard? "The Bard" is a term of respect and endearment for the great English playwright William Shakespeare, whose work contains a lot of memorable quotes. One of those gems is, "To thine own self be true," spoken by Polonius in *Hamlet* (Act 1, Scene 3). Now Polonius is really a pompous windbag who has been a pretty terrible parent, but this "do as I say, not as I do moment" with his son Laertes provides a great quote. Know yourself first and then be true to yourself. Identify your big rocks and then build on them. Walk the talk. Why was Jesus so hard on the religious leaders of his day, the Pharisees and Sadducees? Because they were hypocrites. The self-satisfaction, self-aggrandizement, and self-preservation they exhibited are traps for people in power. Whether it's the Pharisees, the Congress, or the White House, we have to keep in mind the old saying, "Power corrupts. Absolute power corrupts absolutely" (Lord Acton, 1887).

If you are really true to yourself, you will own your imperfections, you will confess your sins, and you will understand it's not about you. The best way to be true to yourself is to live for a cause greater than yourself. Of course, I think the highest cause is the cause of Christ. That can manifest in many ways, and you can connect with a passion. Maybe you can build houses for Habitat for Humanity (I can't do that. I have a finite number of fingers and hands, and I am not good with tools!), or you could donate food for a food pantry, be a bell ringer for the Salvation Army, or package meals for Kids Against Hunger. You can even just make it your life's work to be kind to people.

Wherever your path takes you, please carry the oracle and the Bard with you. Know thyself and to thine own self be true.

Day 5:
I Know that my Redeemer Lives

"I know that my Redeemer lives." These words, spoken by Job in the midst of his suffering, are the words that continue to cycle through my head today. No matter what challenges come the believer's direction, the certainty exists that God lives, God loves, and God is in control. External circumstances do not determine internal peace. Rabid pursuit of the world's "happiness" cannot deliver true joy. Job knew this, the Apostle Paul knew this, and every modern Christian needs to know this.

My mom knew that our Redeemer lives. She was steadfast in her faith, and I remember her saying many times, "God is looking out for our family." He certainly was looking out for us when my mom, dad, foster brother, niece, and I were stranded in a nasty blizzard in 1984. A trucker picked us up when we went off the road, and God used us to save him as much as he saved us. His truck got stuck in a drift, his heat failed around midnight, and our body heat kept us alive as the wind howled all night, gusting to 70 MPH. The six of us had a range of ailments from low body temperature to frostbite to pneumonia when snowmobiles made it out to us at 10:00 A.M. Once a dozen stalled cards had been dragged aside and a special plow from Marshalltown cleared the way for the ambulance, we were out of danger. I was thankful to be able to play four basketball games the following week of my senior year, and my mom's quiet insistence, "God is looking out for our family," was forever cemented in my belief. I know that my Redeemer lives.

On March 28, 1999, Palm Sunday, my Redeemer lived, too. My dad was killed when a car ran a stop sign and drove out onto the highway in front of the min van Dad was driving. My mom was ejected from the vehicle, thrown into a field, and paralyzed. A family friend had her leg crushed. My three nephews and my niece (yes, the same one from the blizzard fifteen years earlier when she was a baby) escaped with their worst injury being a broken collarbone.

Mom did not really have time to grieve Dad in the weeks immediately following the accident because her own life hung in the balance. She had surgery to fuse vertebrae and stabilize her neck. Though she would have to wear a halo brace for months and would be wheelchair bound the rest of her life, she regained some use of her hands. Because she did not have muscle control of her diaphragm muscles and she was bed-ridden, Mom contracted pneumonia and had to struggle for every breath. She was on a ventilator for some time. Through it all, she knew her Redeemer lived.

When Mother Mary could talk, she spoke of what a blessing it was that the children had escaped almost unscathed and that Dad had died instantly and not suffered.

She knew her Redeemer lived. My siblings and I agreed that our mom was better equipped to handle the hospitalizations and challenges she had coming than our dad would have been.

The Iowa Falls Times Citizen ran a big story on my mom with the headline, "Why Not Me?" and that summed up her faith and acceptance so well. My mom knew that the God of the mountains is the God of the valleys, too. She knew that her Redeemer lived and that He loved her. Rather than ask, "Why me?" my mom, in her humility, accepted what happened and replied, "Why not me?"

I could devote a lot of pages to my mom's strength and faith. I could share many stories of how she became more independent even as she became wheelchair bound and reliant on others to provide her care. I could tell you about how she faced four types of cancer head-on, defying the prognosis of four months to live and living four more years. Let me leave it at this: I know that my Redeemer lives, in part, because I witnessed my mother's faithfulness; and I saw God's power, love, and grace in everything she did for many years. I hope that you have had an opportunity to know and love a saint like my mom, whom I know is part of that "great cloud of witnesses" watching over us (Hebrews 12:1).

Day 6:
The Puritan Work Ethic

First big challenge with the book—it's the beginning of a daunting Monday morning, and I don't have the pad I've been writing on with me. It's comical really: I write it all long hand then take five times as long to hunt and peck my way through word processing later. This method does give me time to think, though.

This morning my "Daily Bible Verse" Smartphone widget delivered Acts 20:35: "In all things I have shown you that by working hard in this way we must help the weak and remember the words of the Lord Jesus, how he himself said, 'It is more blessed to give than to receive.'"

I know I previously wrote about work as a Big Rock (Day 2), but I can't think of a better Monday morning topic than work. I believe it's critical that we do the right kind of work, too. In my mind that means doing God's work no matter what your day job is. Martin Luther King, Jr., said it more eloquently than I ever could: "If a man is called to be a street sweeper, he should sweep streets even as Michelangelo painted, or Beethoven composed music, or Shakespeare wrote poetry. He should sweep streets so well that all the hosts of heaven and earth will pause to say, 'Here lived a street sweeper who did his job well.'"

I really believe the truth of that quote, and I appreciate to no end the people who bring spirit to what others might consider menial labor or service jobs. I am very thankful that I have years of restaurant work, grocery bagging, detasseling, and bean walking in my past. Labor is a noble thing, and working to achieve something is always more meaningful than having it given to you (The only danger I see in that statement is for the people who think they can earn salvation, which is the most precious no-strings-attached gift of all time). The Bible urges us to have the right attitude toward work, too. Colossians 3:23 tells us, "Whatever you do, work at it with all your heart, as working for the Lord."

The Puritans certainly knew work as they tried to eke out an existence in the New World. They were an austere bunch, and I'm not sure I'd hire a Puritan as an event planner, but they understood work. I remember an American lit. class in college, circa 1985, when the Puritan Work Ethic was discussed. Because I am a compulsive note-taker, I remember summing up the PWE (had to use an acronym, love those in education) in three short statements: 1. Work for God. 2. Work for others. 3. Work for yourself. I'm sure that's what the points were, and if you gave me some time, I could find the 1985 notebook they are written in, much to my wife's chagrin.

There are times as a school administrator and pastor that I feel I answer to everyone and that my time is not my own. It seems I am always working for others. You can mentally insert, "Duh, did you not know what you were signing up for?" at this point. Of course, I understand these are service occupations. It's just that my selfish human nature makes me feel sorry for myself sometimes. Maybe if the Bears hadn't lost by two on a failed two-point conversion yesterday, I'd feel better. Oh, wait, I did watch almost a whole football game after preaching yesterday. I guess I do make time for myself. Let me return to my point for a minute, though: I answer to everyone, and my time is not my own. <u>Exactly</u>. I do answer to everyone, and so do you. We are part of God's creation, and we should have concern for the rest of God's creation. Our time, all 86,400 seconds a day (Google "The Value of Time" + 86,400 seconds if you want a story to reinforce this idea.) is a gift from God. Each and every day we should endeavor to use it to the fullest.

I have always been a guy who benefited from lists and keeping it simple (KISS- bonus acronym). Sometimes less is more. If only I had a clear plan for using those 86,400 seconds each day! Oh, wait, PWE, 1985:

1. Work for God.

2. Work for others.

3. Work for yourself.

There you have it. Now get to work!

Day 7:
You Can't Manage Time

Ask teachers anywhere what they need more of, and money <u>won't</u> be the first answer; time <u>will</u> be. Teachers probably aren't unique in that regard, at least in the Western World. Our calendars and cell phone clocks drive us relentlessly, from one meeting to the next and one crisis to the next. I will admit that being late or "off schedule" is absolutely a pet peeve of mine, and I should learn to relax a bit.

Time isn't viewed the same way everywhere. My wife, who has been on multiple mission trips to the Southern Hemisphere, (Honduras, El Salvador, Haiti) tells me they have a different view of time in the warmer climes. "In a half an hour" is a common scheduling phrase, but half an hour might mean an hour or two or more. People south of the equator seem to be a bit more relaxed about time. I would have some major adjustments to make if I were suddenly transported to Haiti. I just realized that was a "Captain

Obvious" statement because the concept of time would be just one of many huge adjustments.

God doesn't view time the same way either. The Bible says 1,000 years is like a day to Him (2 Peter 3:8, Psalm 90:4). It also says He has stamped eternity on our hearts (Ecclesiastes 3:11), which is why I think we sense that things are out of balance or lacking harmony when we are getting dogged by our ridiculous schedules. Busy people need to find a way to enforce some quiet time. This book is my personal effort to do that.

The idea for this particular entry came from a "Tuesday Tip" email from Dr. Alan Zimmerman. Ironically, it was titled "Time Management *Strateies*." I resisted the urge to fire off a reply about the importance of reserving time for editing. I really am going to push back against the idea of time management a little because I believe, as I read once (probably in a John Maxwell book), "You can't manage time. You can only manage yourself." I made that exact comment to a young lady in a small group discussion at a minister's retreat. She was feeling great angst because time felt so fleeting to her. Nothing we do can change our appointed time on earth, but how we manage ourselves can definitely affect how we experience that time.

As everyone knows, time on this earth is finite, and it will probably never feel like we have enough of it. Because we never have enough time to do everything, we have to make choices. I think the old dramatic comedy "M*A*S*H," which I faithfully watched during my Wartburg years and still occasionally catch on TV Land, illustrates this concept well. One second Hawkeye and Trapper (or later B.J.) are in the "Swamp" toasting homemade hooch, and the next second Radar O'Reilly's distinctive Ottumwa, Iowa, born voice is beckoning them to their makeshift OR. These battlefield doctors have to make instant life and death decisions about what casualties to treat first. The bland, euphemistic term for this is *triage*.

Any busy ER doc or EMT on the scene of a disaster would have a similar challenge. Priorities have to be set. Injuries that are life threatening get first priority. A mere broken bone might have to wait. There could be a gravely injured person who is considered "too far gone" too, I suppose. We go through a similar process all of the time, not with lives in the balance usually, but we have to decide between things that are merely urgent and things that are really important.

It is no secret that effective people—for example, effective money managers—have short term and long term goals (probably mid term goals, too). Part of the Superintendent Network Instructional Rounds process is creating a list of reflective questions for the host district. Once the questions are written, we identify high leverage questions and quick wins. High leverage questions are really important. They address the kind of things that can really move a school district forward. They can lead to actions that bring about systemic change. I've heard it said that change in schools is like turning a battleship. Therefore, high leverage does not mean quick wins. Quick wins, or short-range goals, might be achieved tomorrow or next week. They might not change a system right away, but they can help build momentum. Quick wins are important, too.

I have coached teams for whom I had to set really intelligent short term goals and for whom I had to try to arrange quick wins. We had to commit to getting better over time because we had a long way to go. We had to keep our spirits up as we were grinding it out. Does that sound like your personal situation, your team, or your work at all?

If you learn to manage yourself and learn to enjoy the challenges, I guarantee that you will feel less time pressure. Maybe you can even learn to be "content in all things" (Philippians 4:11) like the Apostle Paul. I'm still working on that.

Why don't you take the time right now to identify a couple of quick wins for yourself today? Maybe you can sit down and write a note of appreciation to someone you work with. Maybe you can go give your spouse or child a hug. Then move on and identify your high leverage items. Do you need to get healthier? Are you spiritually stagnant? Are you unfulfilled professionally? Begin to manage yourself instead of thinking you can manage time.

Quick Wins I Can Achieve Today

1.

2.

Have a great day!

Day 8:

A Pound of Flesh

Probably a lot of people have heard the phrase "a pound of flesh" as in, "My stupid boss is demanding a pound of flesh on this project." The connotation is that a heavy price is being exacted, that someone is going to have to pay his due. Shakespeare contributed the phrase to our lexicon in his play *The Merchant of Venice*. Shylock, a Jewish money-lender, lends money to the Christian Antonio and sets the collateral for the loan at a pound of Antonio's flesh. When a bankrupt Antonio defaults on the loan, Shylock demands a pound of flesh from Antonio, who had previously insulted Shylock and spit on him. There are probably multiple lessons here; one that jumps to mind is, "Neither a borrower or a lender be." Many people assume this is a Bible quote though it actually is another one from Polonius in Shakespeare's *Hamlet* (Act 1, Scene 3, Verse 75). However, the Bible has a lot to say about borrowing and lending, prohibiting usury and stating, "The borrower is slave to the lender" (Proverbs

22:7). I would suggest William Blake's poem "A Poison Tree" (See Appendix A) and Jonathan Swift's satirical essay "A Modest Proposal" as thought-provoking readings on the topics of revenge and mercy, too. For whatever reason (possibly work pressures or grogginess from a 3:45 A.M. dose of night time cough and cold medicine) I feel a certain weight on my spirit today, and I am thinking about retribution and mercy. Our world could use more mercy. North Korea certainly showed none when it executed 80 people publicly yesterday for the crimes of watching South Korean films, prostitution, and possessing Bibles. Children were forced to watch as victims with pillowcases over their heads were machine gunned beyond recognition. Iran certainly is showing no mercy to the Christian minister imprisoned in one of the country's most dangerous prisons and denied necessary medication. Egypt is showing no mercy to Christians being persecuted in that country. New Mexico is showing no mercy to an evangelical couple that chose not to photograph the homosexual union of two lesbians. Though New Mexico did not recognize gay marriage or civil unions when this happened and the couple has a private photography business, they were fined for not fulfilling the lesbians' request for their photography services. I don't get it.

Max Lucado writes about "The Heaviness of Hatred" in his book *In the Grip of Grace*. He pens, "Everyone gets wounded, hence everyone must decide: how many payments will I demand?" (151). I think this is a very insightful question. How much silence or distance are we going to punish a loved one with when he/she missteps or commits a perceived sin? How long are we going to carry anger or spite in our hearts, lashing out at or belittling someone because "he deserves it"? Are we going to exact our pound of flesh just because we can? Are we going to water our poison tree with the hope that we can one day see our foe dead beneath it?

Can you imagine what life would really be like if we all got just what we deserved? I have been and still am, periodically, a rotten person. I deserve to be the object of scorn and deserve to be damned for my sins. Thank God I don't get what I deserve! My pound of flesh has been paid as a beaten, bloodied Christ hung upon the cross and gave His last breath: "It is finished" (John 19:30). This didn't happen because God is a celestial Shylock. It happened because He is a righteous God, and there was the debt of sin to be paid. Jesus had to take up His cross so that we could be redeemed and have eternity with God.

My prayer for you and for me is that when we get weighed down with cares, we remember that the victory is already won, the final chapter already written. Also, I pray that we can extend grace to people whether they deserve it or not. I know what you're thinking: "It wouldn't be grace if they deserved it." You are exactly right. We all get better than we deserve. God's blessings to you!

People I know who could use a little grace today:_____
_____

Day 9:

What You Don't Do Is As Important As What You Do

One of the district's teachers, a woman who has a passion for helping others and improving their lives, has begun sharing a daily "Pass It On" quote with her colleagues. Today's quote was from the French playwright Moliere: "It is not only for what we do that we are held responsible, but also for what we do not do." This truth has been something that I have tried to keep as a foundational principle for my practice as a school administrator. I remember one of my superintendent courses at Drake University in which the instructor emphasized that what we are determined not to do as superintendents is as important as what we do. I have really internalized that in my non-negotiables. For example, I simply am not going to lie to people.

There are many situations when it would be convenient and more comfortable to lie or to avoid telling the truth. I understand that a Christian, husband, father, pastor, superintendent, or coach without integrity isn't worth a whole lot, though. The momentary discomfort that the hard truth can cause usually gives way to improved understanding, opening the door to something better, agreeing to disagree, or a parting of ways that needs to happen. You probably have heard, "The truth will set you free" (John 8:32). Believe it. The truth will set you free from the pressure of trying to live a lie and from the expectation of trying to be someone you're not.

As a truth teller, you do not have to be a jerk. It is absolutely possible to have the tough conversations without stripping the other person of his/her dignity. I have had a number of those conversations. Using "I" statements helps. Own your own feelings and resist the temptation to lash out with a bunch of "You! You! You!" generalizations (You drive me crazy, you always do that, you need to…). There are many conversation protocols and types of training out there to help people with this. Fierce Conversations, for example, is good, common sense help with having the hard conversation.

Telling the truth or taking a stand on principle will sometimes have you feeling like you're a tree standing all alone. I like a quote I've heard: "Stand up for what you believe in even if it means standing alone." Isaiah 41:19-20 speaks of God putting the pines in the wasteland for people to see and talk about. Both of those are a little more lyrical than the description I remember from superintendent training: "As a superintendent, you're the only tree in the kennel."

A leader, to a certain extent, needs to get beyond the need to be popular or feel liked. I am not saying leaders should try to be unlikable. Being honest and treating others with dignity should bring respect from others, but there will be people who do not want to hear the truth or who simply do not like the leader, and the leader can't let that get in the way of doing the right thing. Even Jesus, who is "the way, the truth, and the life," (John 14:6) was rejected: "The stone the builders rejected has become the cornerstone" (Psalm 118:2).

I say that I am an open book, and I really try to be. I want to be consistent and predictable. My Big Rocks (Day 2) help me here. I really do not want to do anything that will disgrace my God, my family, or my school! I hope you all have convictions and that you have the strength to live your convictions, in what you say and do and in what you <u>don't</u> say and do.

I will _____, _____, and _____!

I won't _____, _____, or_____!

Day 10:
Things Our Mothers Say

I feel sad for the people who have never had the benefit of loving mothers imparting wisdom and direction to them. I'm sure that I cherish my mother's words even more now that she is gone. Certainly there were times when I was growing up that I had no interest whatsoever in her little gems of wisdom. Mother Mary got a mention on Day 5 with, "God is looking out for our family," but I would like to share a few more memories on the topic of things our mothers say. I invite you to roll your eyes, crack a smile, and remember your own mothers' tidbits.

Circa 1971—Picture a whiny five-year-old, tired but not admitting it, being forced to go to bed, and a mom sitting on the end of the bed singing to him. (Important side note: Mom can't carry a tune in a bucket, and the neighborhood dogs are getting riled up.) Mom's advice to the boy: "You quit crying, and I'll quit singing." Newton's Third Law of Motion comes to mind: "Every action has an equal and opposite reaction."

Circa 1978—Picture a resentful pre-teen, rebelling against his father's "master of the house" status, complaining about a perceived injustice and possibly attempting to play one parent against the other (My mom NEVER fell for that). Mom's wisdom: "If you turn out to be half the man your father is, you'll do well." That was a heck of a blow to my twelve-year-old ego and was even more annoying than the ubiquitous, "If you can't say anything nice, don't say anything at all," that I heard when I badmouthed anyone else.

Circa 1982—Picture a sixteen-year-old with a driver's license, longing for some fun and freedom, getting ready to leave the house. Mom's reminder: "Conduct yourself as a young Christian gentleman." I often fell short of this, but it wasn't because I didn't know what it meant or because the expectation wasn't there.

Date Unknown, Ongoing—Picture a Griswolds-type interaction when a little family pride is called for. (If you have not seen National *Lampoon's Vacation* , go rent it today. Hint: *Christmas Vacation* is strong, too. *European Vacation* and *Vegas Vacation* go the way of sequels that should not have been written.) I seem to remember my mom saying repeatedly, "We're Sathoffs; we don't do that," or "We're Sathoffs; we will do the right thing." There's nothing like a family legacy to live up to. If you want a pretty humorous family history, check out the Ewells in *To Kill a Mockingbird*. Of course, the Bible is loaded with lineage, too, both triumphant and tragic.

Circa 1999-2007—Picture a busy professional with family, work, and cares and concerns of his own, feeling inadequate to help with his mom's challenges and guilty that he can't give more. Maybe he wishes he could stay longer at the hospital. Maybe he feels like he neglected his mom because he only called this week and didn't visit. Maybe he feels guilt yet today because his mother passed away as he and his family headed north to see her on Christmas break. Maybe he struggled to just enjoy the quiet presence of an unresponsive parent, or maybe he didn't always remember to turn everything over to God in prayer. Most likely, he has had a good visit with Mom in her home, a care center, or the hospital (maybe even a meal at Pizza Ranch), but now it is time to leave. Mom's reassurance: "You have a life of your own. Take off now. Thank you for coming. Tell Cindy and the boys I love them."

Please listen to your mom and carry her words with you always.

Day 11:

Live, Laugh, Love

I sit by the fake fireplace, lounging in my recliner with a cup of coffee after some quiet time. I am content but really don't know what to write. Then I see the three words, spelled out in large black letters, mingling with the Willow Angels on the ledge in the living room: "live, laugh, love."

I think of Henry David Thoreau's quotes: "Most men lead lives of quiet desperation and go to the grave with the song still in them," and his explanation of why he went to live on Walden Pond in an effort to simplify his life: "I went to the woods because I wished to live deliberately, to front only the essential facts of life, and see if I could learn what it had to teach, and not, when I came to die, discover that I had not lived." Thoreau was a learner, a scientist as well as a philosopher, and he left a legacy for others with his writing. I didn't set out to write about Thoreau today, but he implored people to, "Simplify! Simplify! Simplify!" and that is where I am today with "live, laugh, love."

There are a lot of little details I could fixate on in my work for the school and even for the church. Sometimes we like the micro view because it is small and safe, and it feels good to cross things off our lists when we complete them. It's a little more unsettling to tackle the macro things on a daily basis, things like servant leadership, continuous improvement, change theory, spiritual growth, etc. These are big, scary concepts that people often would rather not think about. Whether it's the little things or the big things, though, an exclusive focus on the "things," on task completion, can lead to us "missing the forest for the trees" and "leading lives of quiet desperation."

That's why I find wisdom and comfort and direction in those three little words: "live, laugh, love." I view life as a gift, and I intend to live it and enjoy it every day. Like most people, I understand life comes with no guarantees, and it seems to fly by faster every day. So many people I know have so many health challenges, family challenges, and financial challenges right now. I am acutely aware of the blessed life I have. I want to live it and have it mean something. If I were to die tomorrow, I would not die with a lot of regrets about how I live my life today. I thank God every day for the blessings of knowing Jesus Christ, having a wonderful family, and having significant work to do. LIVE!

I have often made the comment, " I am going to enjoy my work." I think we make our own fun through our attitudes, our relationships, and our ability to laugh at ourselves. If you can't see the humor in all of life's annoyances, you will drive yourself nuts. There's truth to that old saying sometimes that we laugh because, if we didn't, we'd have to cry. My laughable moments tend to come when I take myself too seriously, rush around too much, or get my priorities out of whack. I can laugh at myself when I'm trying to rush out the door carrying two bags and a travel mug of coffee (sans lid, of course, because our cupboard gremlins take those like the dryer gnomes take one sock per pair), somehow forgetting that if I turn the knob with the hand containing the cup of coffee, it will also turn, spilling its contents on my bag, slacks, and shoes! That's funny. I can give myself a $500 deductible chuckle and laugh at myself in the pulpit, too. With my family on a mission trip in Haiti, I was preaching in two churches one foggy March Sunday and was in a bit of a rush. I don't know why my older son chose to park his Jeep Commander at the bottom of the hill, nose jutting proudly into the driveway. I don't know why the insanely insistent back up beeper didn't register until it was too late for me to avoid smoking the Jeep. Fortunately, my son's vehicle really didn't suffer. Mine got a new back end to go with the $6,600 front end from a week before when I took out a buck on the way home from a ball game. I have to laugh (and thank Progressive for insuring me).

For having nothing to write today, my hand sure is getting tired. Let me wrap up with "love." I am not an overly emotional person or a hearts and flowers guy though I have watched and enjoyed my share of romantic comedies (read "chick flicks"). Love is central to my life, though. I love my God and I love my family. Nothing is more important. I'm working on loving my fellow man. The Two Great Commandments (Matthew 22:37-40) of Jesus are usually front and center in my life: "Jesus replied: 'Love the Lord your God with all your heart and with all your soul and with all your mind.' This is the first and greatest command-ment. And the second is like it: 'Love your neighbor as yourself.' All the Law and the Prophets hang on these two commandments."

I do struggle, sometimes, to answer, "Who is my neighbor?" just as the original disciples did. I pray that God will continue to give me opportunities to love others and that I won't be blind to those opportunities.

There you have it: LIVE, LAUGH, LOVE. That's a pretty good recipe for us.

Day 12:
Be Busy, Not Busybodies

The Apostle Paul writes to the Thessalonians, the second organized Christian church he started, telling them, "Be busy, not busybodies" (2 Thessalonians 3:11). This was just one part of a longer letter that dealt with a lot of challenges that church was facing, like false teachings and serious misbehavior, but this particular advice is timeless: "Be busy, not busybodies."

Is anything more encouraged and enabled today than being a busybody? We are willing victims as we post albums of pictures on Facebook and opine on Twitter and LinkedIn. We are just a very public society, and barriers that once existed between personal and private lives no longer exist. If you are at least middle aged, you probably remember a time when there was an expectation of privacy on phone conversations (Of course, if you go way back, to the times of party lines and the town operator, this is a different conversation).

Pay phones were enclosed in a phone booth, where the speaker could sit and shut the door. Later, people had to stand, but there was still a little kiosk to speak within. Cell phones have changed all of that.

Now we answer and talk practically anywhere, anytime (yes, even in the bathroom). We neglect face-to-face conversation with the person across the desk or table to speak on the cell phone. We will pay our restaurant check or grocery bill while talking on the cell phone. Expect no pleasantries with the clerk. This is a double-edged sword: not only are we lacking civility and minimizing the person right in front of us, but we are also making public what should be a private conversation, subjecting others to it, often at high volume, whether they are interested or not. I'm not casting stones here; I am as guilty of this behavior as most others are.

Another disturbing manifestation of this trend is the "selfie." I usually refrain from commenting on these electronic self-portraits, ubiquitous on Facebook, because I don't want to encourage narcissistic behavior. "Throwback Thursday" is a permutation of the selfie that I can tolerate since it is fun and healthy to laugh at oneself and look back at what once was. "Selfie Friday" is a travesty, though, a smorgasbord of "Look at me!" I suppose there are people with adoring fans who can't wait for the next picture and people who are so darned good looking that it's a public service to share their image. I just am not a fan of the selfie.

I'm sure I'm a disappointment to the Twitterverse, too, at least to my followers. I do tweet occasionally, usually a quote I've read that I liked. Every now and then I re-tweet an article or sports update. I won't deny that one can reach a huge audience and make new connections through Twitter and other social media. I have established somewhat of a

PLN (personal learning network), mostly because someone took the trouble to create an acronym, and we love acronyms in education. I understand the concept of having a digital footprint and accept that if I ever try to change jobs or spark anyone's interest, they will be Googling my name, checking Facebook, etc.

I see a lot of harm done by people not keeping boundaries. Sexting is a big problem for teens and pre-teens, who really aren't mature enough to handle exposing themselves to others. This stuff isn't foolproof either. Ask the University of Iowa graduate assistant who meant to send solutions to math problems to her students and sent sexually explicit content of herself instead! Snap Chat encourages even more sharing that shouldn't happen because images disappear 10-15 seconds after sending. In theory. What happens if someone takes a picture of the picture, or screen shot, during those ten seconds, though? Uh-oh.

Let's go a little more global for a second. Is anyone troubled by the NSA scanning emails and cell phone calls or by Google saving every email ever sent? Foreign leaders have not been amused by the U.S. government monitoring their personal cell phone calls. Global terror and the Patriot Act, which gave the government sweeping powers after 9/11, have led to an erosion of personal privacy in the name of security. I'm not screaming about my Fourth Amendment rights, and I'm pretty middle-of-the-road here. I can handle taking my shoes off for the TSA workers at the airport, and I personally don't mind letting them look at whatever they can stand to see on a body scan as long as I don't have to wait in line too long. I understand why people get concerned, though. I have taught George Orwell's *1984*, and I don't like the idea of Big Brother tracking me through my cell phone or watching me through my computer or TV. I don't want a microchip implant even if it does contain all of my medical records or track my biomedical needs. That's starting to sound too much like the "mark of the beast"(See *Revelation* 13-14).

Globalization and technology have led to a hyper-connectedness that truly has made the world a global village (Thomas Friedman's *The World is Flat* is a seminal work on the topic). There are many benefits to this, and I do believe in community and connectedness. I just fear that the loss of privacy encourages a world of busybodies. Like the Apostle Paul, I believe there is a lot of important work to be done; and if we are glued to our Facebook newsfeed or hip deep in the latest invasive reality TV show, I am afraid that we might forget to live our own lives. Yes, I am on Facebook, Twitter, and LinkedIn. No, you should not feel compelled to "friend" me. If you do, you risk colossal disappointment. Yes, care about people. Offer compassion. Let them live their lives without constant comment, too, even if they have been suckered into making everything an announcement on the World Wide Web.

Day 13:
Coffee is Life

Before you lambast me for trivializing life, understand that it is early Monday morning and that I have already questioned using one of my precious forty days of writing on the topic of coffee, that amazing, life-giving elixir of life. Let me also note, before I go any further, that the <u>real</u> life-giving elixir is the Living Water that Jesus Christ promises (See John 7:38).

I start most mornings by brewing a pot of fresh ground Starbucks. Today I had a few drinking buddies (coffee, remember) and it was two pots, Burundi, then Anniversary Blend. The smell of fresh ground coffee and the resulting pot of warming goodness is a great way to start the day. I am not really a morning person, and I don't go to bed very early either, so I am sure there is a physiological basis (caffeine) for my loving coffee, too. Probably my brain starts producing dopamine or other endorphins the second the grinder starts whirring. If eating chocolate or posting to Facebook can do that for people, as I've heard, then surely making coffee can, too. I won't get into the science too much here, but as long as my heart can handle 8-12 cups of strong coffee in the morning, my brain and taste buds are all in.

Beyond the pleasant taste, smell, and warmth of coffee and the documented benefits to alertness and mental acuity, coffee has a whole host of positive associations. One of the foremost benefits of coffee is community. Why do you suppose those lovable "Seinfeld" goofballs meet at the coffee shop? I know what you're thinking: there's another lovable "Cheers" crew that meets at a bar, but I'm a non-drinker of thirteen years, and I'm not going to devote Day 14 to "Beer is Life." Coffee is community. How many coffee clubs do you suppose there are in the United States and throughout the world? I know that in rural Iowa Casey's General Store is a de facto coffee club for farmers across the state. I've interrupted a few of those to get a cup for the road when I have been traveling to meetings. I think Hy-Vee deli or the local grain elevator might be common coffee klatches, too. Coffee gives people a reason to get together, and I think anything that gets people face-to-face to talk is a good thing.

Let me tell you a little bit about how I came to be a coffee drinker at age seven. For the record, I am a robust 6'6" so it did not stunt my growth either. My dad was an avid antique-er and lover of small towns, so it was no surprise that he found Roy and Fern Allison in Bradford, Iowa. I suppose Roy and Fern were in their late 70s at least when I was a child of seven, visiting their home, which doubled as an antique shop. Bradford was a little town of maybe 150 people seven miles north of Iowa Falls, where I grew up. I remember my dad referring to a former student from there as the "Mayor of Bradford."

It seems like we usually visited Roy and Fern around suppertime, or at least I remember eating Fern's goulash a number of times. What I really remember is the old stove in the corner, kicking off heat and warming a percolator of strong coffee. Roy and I would sit and have coffee with cream while Mom and Dad dickered with Fern on purchase prices. Roy was a good old boy, always garbed in bibs. For some unfathomable reason, he always chose to call me "Mabel," but he was a good-hearted guy, and he gave me a Cribbage education. I don't stop to reflect very often about the debt of gratitude I owe to Roy for introducing me to Cribbage and coffee.

As I have indicated in other days' writings, I think we do ourselves a disservice if we don't slow down and take the time to be reflective. I think we miss out on a lot of the good stuff of life if we don't interact with or commune with others. A Cribbage board or a cup of coffee is as good a vehicle for that as most other things. The Blue Zones initiative recommends connecting with the right "tribes," too, and specifically mentions church/spirituality as one of the "Power 9" standards for living a long, healthy life. I hope that if you don't have an active church life, for whatever reason, that you will consider giving that a try. Most churches are even smart enough to have a coffee time!

Day 14:
Do It Right the First Time

I can think of so many applications of this day's topic that I don't know where to begin! I really do not like to do things halfway, and if I am going to put my name on something, I want to know I have done the best I can to do it right. I want to insert one big qualifier here, which is that I fully understand and embrace trial and error, risk-taking, and failure if we learn from those things. At the same time I want to "do it right the first time," I understand that life is a process, we are continually growing and learning (hopefully), and failure usually isn't fatal (unless it's failure to pull the rip cord, failure to bring a life jacket, failure to remember your anniversary, etc.). Acknowledging that caveat, I still do not want to be like the cook who proudly displayed a sign that read, "I am not a fast cook. I am not a slow cook. I am a half fast cook."

Restaurant work is actually a pretty good place to illustrate today's topic. I draw on my vast experience as an employee of the Red Rooster, Gene's on Main, Allison Dairy Sweet, and Mike's Prairie Home. I also like to watch "Mystery Diners" and "Restaurant Stakeout." If the wait staff doesn't get the order written correctly the first time, the food preparers are doomed. If the cooks don't get the order prepared right, the wait staff is in a jam. Sometimes there might be an easy fix for the problem. If a steak ordered medium comes out a little "under" at medium rare, that can be easily fixed although I've seen enough gross movie scenes (I'm thinking of the French toast in *Road Trip*, I think), that I'm a little nervous about sending food back. If food comes out with hair in it, that's pretty hard to fix. The appetite is gone! If customers have to wait an hour for their food, there might not be a second chance to get it right. Ability to do the job, adequate resources and personnel to get the job done, and customer service are important. All of these things contribute to doing it right the first time in a restaurant.

As a coach, I know I always really appreciated the athletes that watched and listened carefully and tried to perform the skill exactly as described and demonstrated. Even if things didn't turn out exactly as planned, their effort to do it right the first time was a step toward ingraining positive habits and creating muscle memory. The exasperating athletes were the ones who had the physical ability, nodded their way through a practice or time out, then went and did their own thing, often to the detriment of the team. There are employees like this, too. The question that arises for a coach or supervisor at this time is, "Are you stupid or stubborn?" I do not recommend actually asking that question, at least in those terms. Just mull it over. Does the person really not understand, in which case the coach/supervisor has to maintain a consistent message while trying to coach/teach another way, or is the person willfully disregarding the direction? In that case the coach/supervisor must either sell them on the message or force them into compliance. I think you can tell which one of those two things is preferred. Be wary of those who give lip service without accompanying action. Remember the parable of the two sons in Matthew 21:28-31:

"What do you think? There was a man who had two sons. He went to the first and said, 'Son, go and work today in the vineyard.'

'I will not,' he answered, but later he changed his mind and went.

Then the father went to the other son and said the same thing.

He answered, 'I will, sir,' but he did not go.

'Which of the two did what his father wanted?'

'The first,' they answered."

I encourage everyone to be organized, visualize intended outcomes, and work hard for desired results. Things will not always turn out as planned, and there are many things beyond our control. At those times it is useful to remember "The Serenity Prayer," which reads, "God grant me the serenity to accept the things I cannot change; the courage to change the things I can; and the wisdom to know the difference." I guess what I am really advocating is balance. Make every effort to get it right the first time, but don't drive yourself crazy when you don't.

What project(s) do you have coming up that you really need to get right the first time? _____

_____

Day 15:

Appreciation

Appreciation is probably today's topic because whenever I am at my most tired or busy state, I need to stop and remind myself how good I have it. I got home at 1:00 A.M. last night after a double overtime basketball game in Lamoni, Iowa. Believe me, I <u>appreciated</u> that our son's team, the Graceland University Yellowjackets, won and that I was able to swerve around the big deer lying dead in my lane on Highway 34 on the way home. My wife didn't necessarily appreciate being wakened by my jerking the wheel at that moment, and I certainly wasn't appreciating or respecting the "Don't veer for deer advice," but I don't know if that goes for dead deer, and I definitely did appreciate not being stranded with a broken axle on our one reliable vehicle at midnight.

I also appreciated that the basketball coach, who lets me volunteer with the high school program when I can get there, gave me a pass on 6:15 A.M. practice. That allowed me to sleep until 6:20 and still make it to serve the Staff Appreciation Breakfast at 7:00 A.M. for American Education Week. I really appreciated it when an associate I worked with for a couple of years at the high school said, "You are adorable," when I picked up her tray. The "only tree in the kennel" does not get described as adorable all that often!

I certainly appreciate my wife. "My lovely bride," as I often calls her, and I are approaching 24 years of wedded bliss. She got up early this morning, too, since we are down two vehicles right now, to drop me off at the school. She also had me organized, bag packed, to be on the road Wednesday through Saturday.

Tonight I will have dinner in Des Moines with our full board of education and our school business official. Tomorrow we will be at the state school board convention together. I deeply appreciate that I have had boards that commit a lot of time to their important volunteer leadership role and boards that have been willing to work and learn together. I am truly blessed to work with an outstanding administrative team, teaching staff, and support staff, too. The emails of appreciation I received after this morning's breakfast were uplifting as well.

From the school board convention I go straight to Ames to serve as a board member myself for the Iowa High School Music Association Executive Board. This is All-State Festival weekend, and Fairfield has a number of qualifying participants. There's another thing I appreciate: Fairfield CSD's awesome vocal and instrumental programs and directors (not to mention speech, drama, athletics, FBLA, FFA, etc.)!

I feel appreciation because I am blessed, plain and simple. I am very busy, but I am busy with the right things. I often have people say to me, "I don't know how you do everything you do," but I know. As the well-known Philippians 4:13 says, "I can do all things in Christ, who strengthens me." I think as long as we're doing God's work, He will give us an endless reservoir of energy to tap into.

When I return home from Ames after the concert Saturday, arriving around midnight, I will go to bed knowing I will be up early Sunday to serve as an elder at Packwood Christian Church and then go preach at Fairfield First Christian Church. These church families are a blessing to my family, and we are very thankful for them. I will head into Thanksgiving week next week already feeling very thankful because God is using me and letting me do what I love to do. I feel like I am being faithful with what He has given me, and I think of the promise of Matthew 25:29: "For whoever has will be given more, and they will have an abundance. Whoever does not have, even what they have will be taken from them." I know which side of that equation I want to be on.

In *Meditations* great Roman writer and statesman Marcus Aurelius wrote, "Dwell on the beauty of life. Watch the stars, and see yourself running with them." I like that, but I also think there is a great deal of beauty in our average, everyday activities, and I hope we appreciate that!

What are the things or people you appreciate most in life? List them here, and consider writing the people responsible a note of appreciation.

I appreciate. . .

1.

2.

3.

4.

Day 16:

Discipline

The word *discipline* gets applied in numerous contexts, many of them negative. *Corrective* discipline, *employee* discipline, *student* discipline, *disciplinary* measures—these are all examples of how the word gets attached to people or actions in a punitive way. For many the word *discipline* is synonymous with, or a euphemism for, *punishment*. It is interesting how word meanings change through the years. As an old English teacher, I used to teach denotation and connotation, the literal and emotional meanings of words. We also studied amelioration and pejoration, how words attain more positive or more negative meanings over time. These things are in play with the word *discipline*, which has as its root *disciple*: a learner, a follower.

Jesus was, of course, the greatest rabbi, or teacher, ever. He used parables to make learning real. He rebuked His disciples when they needed it. "Get behind me, Satan!" he said to Peter (Matthew 16:23) when Peter lacked understanding of God's plan and "You of little faith!" (Matthew 8:26) when His disciples feared the storm. Most of all, he equipped them for the trials they had ahead and to fulfill the Great Commission to, " go and make disciples of all nations," (Matthew 28:19), which believers still have a responsibility to do today.

Jesus didn't sugar coat things with his disciples. He told them multiple times that He would have to suffer and die at the hands of the religious leaders but that God would raise Him from the dead (Matthew 26:24, Mark 8:31, Luke 9:22). They didn't understand. They wanted an earthly king. Jesus told them if they really wanted to follow Him, they would have to take up their cross and follow Him (Matthew 16:24). He asked them, "Can you drink from the cup I am going to drink from?" (Matthew 20:22), and they thought they could, but they had a lot to learn. Jesus knew that they would face persecution, hardship, and death, and He wanted them to be ready.

We need to be ready, too. We need to be continually learning and striving to grow. Certain things have to happen for us to continually learn and grow, though. These things are often called *disciplines*, too. There are spiritual disciplines, such as prayer, worship, and Bible study. There are personal disciplines, such as exercise, hard work, and relationship building.

I have found my greatest personal growth comes through the disciplines in my life. One of the first steps on this path came for me over 13 years ago when I decided I was no longer going to drink alcohol. I wasn't a raging alcoholic. I didn't <u>need</u> to decide that. I just thought, as our children were growing up and I was entering school administration, that abstaining would be a good example to set and a good discipline for me. I have been happy with the decision.

Another discipline, which has been extremely valuable to me, has been the practice of note-taking. I am a copious note-taker. I describe myself as a compulsive note-taker. As a student I took a lot of notes (probably to stay awake). Beyond my formal education, I have gotten into the practice of taking notes on anything I read (unless it is purely for pleasure, like a newspaper, magazine, or mystery novel). I'm sure I have legal pads full of notes all over the place that will never see the light of day again. Every now and then I go back and find a gem, though, and I guarantee that I learn more and internalize more when I write it down. My work is complex enough and my memory bad enough that note taking is very beneficial!

Writing this book has been a discipline. I am writing every day for 40 days, and I am writing just one entry a day. I am finding this undertaking to be extremely valuable personally, and I hope others will benefit from it, too.

I have a habit of writing a personal birthday card to every school district employee. This is a discipline. I have to schedule time to do it. Even with a modest number of employees, under 300, there are weeks with up to ten employee birthdays, and I might be out of the district several times that week. I'm not going to just skip those birthdays. I want people to know they are remembered and appreciated.

I love the book of Proverbs and all it has to say about discipline. Proverbs 12:1 says, "Whoever loves discipline loves knowledge." Proverbs 15:32 says, "Those who disregard discipline despise themselves." Proverbs 23:13 reminds us, "Do not withhold discipline from a child." Believe me, I've seen the results of that last one as a school administrator! Discipline is for our own good. If we embrace learning and personal development, we can grow, and God can use us in ways we never imagined. We have to be open to change. We have to understand that discipline is not about comfort.

Coaches will pretty universally tell you that growth occurs when athletes "get out of their comfort zone." Everyone has heard, "No pain, no gain." Most of us have offered the advice that you get out of something what you put into it. That is easy-to-give advice for others, but let's remember it is good for us, too.

I used to have a poster from the Iowa High School Athletic Association hanging in my classroom that read, "We are what we repeatedly do. Excellence, then, is not an act but a habit." The quote was attributed to Aristotle. Take a minute right now and think about what good habits you could start, what disciplines you need to focus on. You won't be sorry.

- Here are a few suggestions:
- Tell your family you love them every day.
- Write notes of appreciation every day.
- Begin and end your day with prayer and reflection.
- Get some physical activity every day.
- Read the Bible every day.
- Always have at least one good book in progress.

Day 17:

Develop Your Talents

The Iowa High School All-State Music Festival provides a perfect backdrop for today's writing. This weekend in Ames the state's most talented high school vocalists and instrumentalists will gather in Hilton Coliseum for a breath-taking concert. They will spend the days leading up to the concert practicing together, and they have spent the weeks, months, and years prior to that honing their God-given gifts.

We all have talents; we all have gifts. Too often we focus on what we can't do and engage in negative self-talk. The greatest limitations in our lives are self-imposed. We all have different talents and gifts. That's the way God intends it. There is remarkable variety in the natural world and in the human race. As the saying goes, "Variety is the spice of life." Within each one of us there is a variety of gifts and abilities waiting to be developed.

We have a responsibility to use and develop our gifts. This is merely good stewardship, making the most of what we have been given. I really am not speaking about "self-made men" or "pulling ourselves up by our bootstraps," though. I think these phrases focus on work to the exclusion of gift-edness. What I am speaking of is more of an awareness of where God has given us passion and ability, and the willingness to use that passion and ability for good, for others' benefit.

As I was growing up, I worked very hard to develop talents God had given me. I participated in the All-State weekend I now attend as a board member when I was a singer in 1984. I was an All-State basketball player who set State Tournament records and was inducted into the Iowa Basketball Hall of Fame. I was a state speech and state track qualifier, had the lead in our school musical, and participated in student government and National Honor Society. I have a lot of good memories, and I wouldn't go back and undo the hard work or accomplishments. I would go back and enjoy the process more as developing my gifts and giving the glory to God rather than focusing on awards and accolades and seeing what I could accomplish for me. I care less about that today, and that's how I end up as a pastor, volunteer coach, and board member in addition to my job as superintendent. I also have more joy in being Christian, husband, and father than any title.

The really significant people—Jesus Christ, the Apostle Paul, Mother Teresa, Mahatma Gandhi, Nelson Mandela, Martin Luther King, Jr.—you can mentally construct your own list, developed their gifts in the service of others and changed the world! We can do that one person at a time by extending kindness, praying for people in need, offering a smile or helping hand, and showing God's love. There will be hardships and inconvenience in doing so. Anything worth doing takes effort.

I hope that you recognize you are a child of God, made just the way He wants you. You probably have hidden talents waiting to be developed. If you have already discovered your passion and gifts, use them. And use them in the service of others. I admire the career of John Maxwell, minister turned leadership expert and author. His passion, as he often says, is "adding value" to others. To whom do you add value? Hopefully everyone you come into contact with.

1. We all have talents and gifts from God.

2. We all have different talents and gifts.

3. We have a responsibility to use and develop our gifts to add value to the world.

Have a great day!

Day 18:

Own Your Mistakes

I have made more than my share of mistakes. I have acted thoughtlessly and recklessly. I have hurt other people and myself. I own my mistakes.

I remember the "Order of Confession and Forgiveness" that was part of the liturgy in Bethany Lutheran Church in Iowa Falls, where I grew up. I think it hits the nail right on the head: "We confess that we have sinned against You in thought, word, and deed, by what we have done and by what we have left undone. We have not loved You with our whole heart. We have not loved our neighbors as ourselves." Those statements <u>convict</u> me. My prayer is the prayer of the publican, or tax collector: "Lord have mercy on me, a sinner" (Luke 18:13).

I title today's entry "Own Your Mistakes" because I think our response to our mistakes, or sins, matters. Of course, this line of reasoning supposes recognition of wrongdoing, and many people work overtime to minimize or deflect any such recognition. They rationalize improper behavior ("I did not have sex with that woman, Miss Lewinski."), blame it on others, deny it ("It depends on what the definition of 'is' is."), or refuse to recognize any moral standard that condemns them. How often does someone say, "It's personal," or "Respect my privacy," when there is immoral behavior? I pray for the person who has never felt convicted like the publican and me because really, he/she is just an unrepentant sinner.

Once the behavior is recognized, we can go about the business of learning and rebuilding. People can be such slow learners, making the same mistakes again and again! It is hard work replacing bad habits or breaking the cycle of destructive behavior. We need help practicing what Rick Warren calls the principle of "removal and replacement." Even when we know better, it is difficult. Sin is beguiling.

As a principal I always appreciated the kid who admitted, "I screwed up," without a lot of prompting. With that student I could re-purpose a whole bunch of investigative time and energy into building better relationships and decision-making skills. The conversation became more about personal growth and lessons learned than punishment. I once had reported to me a student comment: "I don't like getting sent to the office because then Mr. Sathoff talks to you." I didn't try to talk people into submission, but I did try to make them think and own their own behavior.

I also really appreciated a comment I got from a teacher when I was a principal. As her supervisor I was flattered to hear, "We all want to do our best job because we don't want to disappoint you." I understand there's a little bit of a paternalistic model there, which can be another problem, but I think most leaders would appreciate hearing that.

As parents we look forward to those days when our children will do the right thing because they don't want to disappoint us and because they know what's right, not because they want to avoid getting into trouble. There's a great little exchange between Jem and Scout on this in Harper Lee's *To Kill a Mockingbird*. That's a book to put on your reading list if you have never read it.

God must feel a great deal of joy when we try to lead lives that would please Him. He has put His law in our minds and written it on our hearts (Jeremiah 31:33), so we know what moral behavior is. Keeping the law or doing good works, though, doesn't save us. Our Christian behavior comes from our gratitude for the awesome gift of grace we receive!

John Maxwell's book *Sometimes You Win, Sometimes You Learn* does a great job of exploring how we learn from our own failures. Taking responsibility is the first step. I urge all of us to practice the art of honest, humble acceptance of our mistakes. Then we can get about the business of picking up the pieces, learning from our mistakes, and growing as human beings. In the words of country artist Tim McGraw, "I ain't as good as I'm gonna get, but I'm better than I used to be."

Day 19:

Traveling

How do you feel about traveling? You know, I really like going places, but I'm not sure I care much for traveling. This past week I got my share. Tuesday after school Cindy and I took the manageable two hour-fifteen minute trip each way to see Trey play basketball in scenic Lamoni, Iowa. After a double overtime game, a win at least, the trip home from 10:30 P.M.-12:45 A.M. felt a lot different than the trip there. Wednesday night after work the two-hour trip to downtown Des Moines was a breeze. The thirty miles from Des Moines to Ames the next afternoon was not one bit of fun in the freezing rain. By the time I got started home at 10:00 P.M. Saturday night, a two-plus hour trip felt like a hardship, especially when I had to battle post-concert and Cyclone football traffic and police barricades just to get out of town. I was beat by the time I got home at 12:30 A.M. You know, sometimes I long for a "Star Trek" teleportation device, or transporter. If I can't get that, a "Jetsons" personal spaceship would at least help!

In case you are starting to feel sympathetic, don't. It's all self-inflicted, and travel has given me awesome experiences and memories of Germany (East <u>and</u> West before "The Wall" fell), Amsterdam, Argentina, Australia, Ireland (kissed the Blarney Stone twice), Hawaii (two trips to different islands), and Mexico (at an all-inclusive resort). That's not bad for a small-town son of a schoolteacher whose family vacations growing up were the Vagabond Motel (with tiny outdoor pool on University Avenue in Cedar Falls) with breakfast at Sambo's and lunch at Big Boy. We did eventually graduate to Adventureland and were there its opening season, when it had one tiny roller coaster and a few other notables like the log ride and bumper cars.

In my adult life, I don't regret a single mile traveled through a decade of AAU basketball and college basketball for our two boys. We have seen everything from Thanksgiving and Christmas tournaments in blizzards in Eau Claire, Wisconsin, to scorching hot white sand at Cocoa Beach, Florida. We made our own fun in Cocoa Beach, "crabbing" with the Spielbauers. Florida Governor Jeb Bush even sent all of our players lifetime crabbing licenses (I should have been a forger). Most of our AAU destinations weren't that glamorous. Sites like Kearny, Nebraska; Sioux Falls, South Dakota; Orange City, Iowa; and Northfield, Minnesota, seem to outnumber trips to Florida, Las Vegas, and Hawaii.

These were our family vacations, though: wracking up the miles, spending the day in a gym, alternating between begging and threatening the two boys sharing a bed to shut up so I could get enough sleep to get us home safely the next day. There are lots of great basketball memories as both a coach and a parent, roles Cindy enjoyed, too, through the years.

Once Jordan was done playing AAU and Cindy was working full-time, there were a couple of springs and summers when it was usually just Trey and I on the road. We got a lot of good windshield time together. It wasn't all spent in deep conversation though it was bonding time. Sometimes guys aren't great at talking. Women do more talking. Men play or watch games together. Unfortunately for my bruised arm and me, Trey was a lot better at the Slug Bug game than I was. We expanded it to cover a lot of other things, too, like punching on yellow vehicles ("Banana Slap") as well as "Jeeper Beeper," "Ram Jam," and other calls. In case you aren't following this, whoever sees and calls out the designated vehicles first gets to punch the other person. I had to pay some attention to the road, and I was older and slower than Trey, so I took a beating. I knew, though, that Trey would sleep sometime, and I would have the opportunity to count and save up some slugs for him. Immature? Certainly, but it is a bond and a shared history we have, too.

Now Cindy and I make it to every Graceland Yellowjackets game we can. Before that it was Wartburg Knights games. We're getting to know Kansas, Missouri, and Nebraska backroads pretty well. "Heart of America Athletic Conference" sounds kind of exciting and inspiring, but most of the destination cities are pretty ordinary. Last year we only missed one game (Baldwin City, Kansas, on an icy, frigid week night) and hit one deer (a trophy buck I did not stop to get the rack from between Chariton and Albia) in piling up over 11,000 basketball miles. This year we already have missed two games in Florida, but we did buy Jordan a plane ticket to go support his brother and visit his uncle's family in Daytona Beach. What was I doing? Re-read paragraph one of Day 19.

I really don't think I would appreciate the destinations like I do without the travel, earlier longing for transporters and spaceships aside. Every wrong turn, delay, storm, restaurant, gas station, gym, late night, and early morning has a story and a memory. Is it any wonder that we talk about the "journey of life"? In fact, we come to understand that life is the journey; life is what happens to us when we're on the way to where we're going. There are destinations, and we are just visitors and travelers here. Our journeys provide a wonderful preparation for us. They communicate what's important to us and what we love.

I think of all the traveling I do. It's worth it to me to drive to Packwood to worship and serve as an elder before I drive back home to Fairfield to preach. I'm traveling for my Big Rock of Faith, spending time in worship with the family of God and sharing His Word. It's worth it to me to sacrifice sleep and money and drive the wheels off our vehicles to support our sons and share the game of basketball with them. I'm traveling for my Big Rock of Family. It's worth it to me to do the extras for my job, attending conferences and training and events around the state. I'm traveling for my Big Rock of Work. When we know why we are striving for something, sacrificing for it becomes worthwhile.

I wish you safe travels and a fulfilling journey in this life, and I hope you are certain of your final destination!

Day 20:
Whom do you listen to?

Okay, let me give you a little context for what's going on in my pea-sized brain today. Ralph Waldo Emerson, American Transcendental philosopher and author of the essay "Self Reliance," and John Donne, English Metaphysical poet and author who penned, "No man is an island entire of itself," are having a little debate within my skull. Really the debate is already settled because we all hear voices, some more than others, running through our brains. I suggest country artist Chris Young's song "Voices" for a happy version of this. I believe the extent to which we practice positive self-talk is a strong predictor of our ability to effect positive change in our own lives and the lives of others. You have heard slogans like, "If you believe, you can achieve," and terms like "self-fulfilling prophecy." Dr. Norman Vincent Peale famously wrote about "The Power of Positive Thinking." In education we stress the importance of *self efficacy* and *collective efficacy*, the belief that an individual and a group can succeed. I am not a touchy-feely Stuart Smalley self-affirmer. That's a shout out to classic SNL ("Saturday Night Live"). In the Stuart Smalley sketch the character looks into a mirror and says, "I'm good enough, I'm smart enough, and gosh darn it, people like me." Bonus Poet Alert: As English author John Milton wrote in *Paradise Lost*, "The mind is its own place, and in itself can make a heaven of hell, a hell of heaven." I also believe Viktor Frankl has a lot to offer on this topic in his book *Man's Search for Meaning*.

I am not writing merely about attitude here but about listening to the interior monologue that plays throughout our every waking moment, usually in the background. Actually, our subconscious probably speaks to us, too, when we aren't awake, but I'm not prepared to tackle that. Let me tell you a few of the voices I listen to:

1. My body—I am generally healthy though not a fitness fanatic. I know what my old, arthritic knees can take. They tell me. I know when I've been sedentary and eating too much. Both my fat gut and the scale keep me informed. I know when even my fresh ground Starbucks can't me in the groove because I'm sleep deprived. My caffeine-resistant headache says, "Hey, knucklehead, you'd better find a way to get to bed early tonight." I'm sure your body speaks to you, too. If you listen a little along the way, you might prevent a big collapse.

2. My parents—I certainly wish that every person had caring, loving parents who weren't too distracted, too self-absorbed, or too wishy-washy to parent. If people have these parents, they should listen to them. My parents passed away in 1999 and 2007, but I still hear their words to me. They did so much to shape and influence me, and I am eternally grateful. The wisdom

of grandparents, aunts and uncles, and older siblings could be included here, too. Let's not forget that we have a loving Father in Heaven whom we most certainly should be striving to listen to as well.

3. My spouse—Hopefully it will not be too much of a surprise to my lovely bride that she shows up on this list. My wife Cindy has shaped my life and influenced me as much as any other single person. I listen to her because she has the right values, she is smart and caring, and she is always going to say exactly what she thinks. Her other family members, her co-workers, and her friends would tell you the same thing. As we parented together, coached together, and grew together, I think Cindy and I began to see the world more and more through the same lens. If I need to check my thinking, to see what I <u>should</u> be thinking, Cindy is the person to talk to.

4. Sounding boards—Most of us need sounding boards. In my school administration career I have been blessed with <u>awesome</u> secretaries and administrative colleagues. When I do need to vent, whine, do a tone check on something, or ask advice, these people in my professional life are so valuable! As a superintendent, I value my board president as a great sounding board, too. I'm thankful for the good head she has on her shoulders and for her willingness to listen.

5. Accountability partners—I think we need these, too, because human beings are not inherently disciplined creatures. My wife Cindy would function as my exercise accountability partner (and my sportsmanship accountability partner when I start yelling at the refs too much). My admin colleagues are professional accountability

partners. They would call, "B.S.!" if I wasn't doing my job or supporting them. The school board is an accountability partner in terms of being a budget watchdog. The two churches I attend and serve remind me of the importance of worship and fellowship. I am accountable to a lot of people, and I like that. It keeps me focused and on track.

6. The still small voice—The voice we should listen to the most is "the still small voice" of 1 Kings 19. Elijah had been on the run for his life, living in caves, and he was looking to God for answers. God came in a great wind that tore rocks from the mountain, but Elijah didn't hear Him. He came in an earthquake, but Elijah didn't note Him. Then a fire came, but Elijah didn't see God in the fire. And then there was **a still small voice**, and Elijah heard it. You know, I think God can speak to us in the big, dramatic events in our lives. I really hope, though, that we can listen carefully for that still small voice. You can call it conscience, Jiminy Cricket, or whatever you want, but I hope you listen. The more we become attuned to God's Will for our lives, the happier we are and the more He can use us.

Take a minute and reflect. What voices are you listening to?

1.

2.

3.

Have a great day and start listening!

Day 21:

Self-assessment

As I was struggling to think of a topic today, I decided I would watch my "Minute with Maxwell" on self-assessment. Every day I get an email with a short video of John Maxwell speaking about a term or concept. Almost always, I put it in an electronic folder without looking at it. Dr Zimmerman's "Tuesday Tip" often gets the same treatment though I do use it at standing meetings with my building staff sometimes. The same is true of Seth Godin's daily blog. Rick Warren's daily devotional I sometimes tap into for a monthly church newsletter idea. As you can see, there is no shortage of good ideas and wisdom out there for us to access.

Today I heard Maxwell reflect on his early days as a counselor, and he said, "Most people do not see themselves accurately." I bet you could make a list right now of people with a skewed self-perception. One of my pet peeves is when people have an exaggerated sense of self-importance, followed closely by people who have a persecution complex. It's not <u>about</u> you, and everyone is not out to get <u>you</u>. I have to give myself those reminders sometimes, too. I acknowledge I've already written about knowing thyself (Day 4) and positive self-talk (Day 20). I don't have 40 unique topics to write about, though. As one of my administrative colleagues told another one in an admin meeting, "You're not that complex." That is certainly true of me.

Why is it important to self-assess? Maxwell says, "I don't trust myself." He recommends finding a friend that unconditionally loves you to come alongside you to help with the task of self-assessment. This is the same concept I suggested with accountability partners. Another thing you could try is a tool called the Yohari Window. I encountered it in a graduate class and have used it with staff a couple of times. There is a detailed model, based on a design by Alan Chapman, at www.businessballs.com . You can very easily make your own Yohari Window for self-assessment purposes.

Draw a four-paned window, a square with a horizontal line and a vertical line down through the middle, creating four quadrants. Title the upper left quadrant the "Public Self." The Public Self is known and agreed upon by you and others. Title the upper right quadrant "Perceived Self." The Perceived Self is unknown by you but known by others. You should solicit feedback on this. I like anonymous surveys and invite every school district employee to evaluate me anonymously. Many people advocate 360 degree feedback, and John Maxwell has a good book called *The 360 Degree Leader*. Title the lower left quadrant the "Hidden Self." This is the area known to you but not to others. Title the lower right quadrant the "Unknown Self." This is the part of you not known by yourself or others. Let me recap those four selves and comment briefly:

1. Public Self—Everyone can agree on this. Your job, status, public reputation, and things that are not in dispute fall into this area. Of course, this quadrant doesn't tell the whole story about anyone. As Henry David Thoreau, a previously quoted author, wrote, "Public opinion is a weak tyrant compared to our own private opinion." There are times we should not accept how our public self defines us, at least not as the totality of who we are. Remember, there are four windowpanes.

2. Perceived Self—This pane is a great reminder to us that we are social creatures, we have an impact on everyone we meet, and we are not always 100 percent aware of that impact. I think most leaders, as they work with people, learn to read people and their reactions. Whether or not we agree with their perception of us is beside the point. I often remind administrators, "Perception is reality." Your perceived self is the reality of who you are to others. Ignore this at your peril.

3. Hidden Self—I have some mixed feelings on this one. I know that many people will say, "I have a right to a private life," or "What I do on my own time is my business." I can't really argue that, but I have been a public figure for a long time, and I have learned that secret lives are more often shameful than laudable. I know there are exceptions, like the people who put valuable gold coins in Salvation Army kettles anonymously or people who lead quiet lives then leave millions to their churches or communities when they die. As I wrote earlier, I strive to be an open book and to have my private and public

self be as close to the same as possible. Sometimes I fail. I think people appreciate it when we are authentic and let them see our hidden self. It is okay to display our vulnerability and fears as well as our passions, as long as we aren't doing an emotion dump on others all of the time. Trying to live in harmony with God's Will for my life, as I discern it from Scripture, prayer, and the Spirit moving in my life, is how I align my private and public lives. After all, there is no hidden self to God. Adam and Eve found that out.

4. Unknown Self—There has to be a little mystery in life. I consider myself to be pretty reflective and self-aware, but sometimes I don't know who the heck I am. At these times I focus on who I am supposed to be. To a large extent it doesn't matter where we're at. What matters is where we're going and what we're capable of becoming. We are all "projects." We will never "arrive" as long as we are in this world. When I grapple with the unknown self, I hold on to what I do know. I am a child of God. He loves me and has great plans for me. I am a husband and father who is incredibly blessed in family. I am a pastor, superintendent, and coach with very important work to do. These are the knowns to answer the unknown.

Have a great day, and happy self-assessing to you! Why don't you sit down and reflect and write on your Yohari windowpanes?

Public Self	Perceived Self
Hidden Self	Unknown Self

Your Yohari Window

Day 22:

Thanksgetting

Today is an experiment to see if I can write solely on the basis of a word I just made up. I have to note that I am going on less than five hours sleep and no coffee. You do remember my previous entry titled "Coffee is Life" (Day 13), right? Fortunately, tomorrow is Thanksgiving, and that gives me good inspiration. So why didn't I just title this "Thanksgiving"? Maybe that will be tomorrow. I just make this stuff up day-by-day.

Do you ever celebrate *thanksgetting*? It can happen any day. I had a moment of thanksgetting this morning when a co-worker who is facing some big health challenges stopped and thanked me for sending her a thoughtful note. This gave me an opportunity to ask if I could lift her up by name for prayers in the churches I attend and serve. That question led to more thansgiving and thanksgetting. Are you seeing a trend here? It's so simple really. I have heard it said that love is the only thing that, the more you give away, the more you have. Do you find yourself feeling unappreciated or underappreciated? Do you feel like you're not getting much thanks? Look in the mirror. How much thanks are you giving? How much appreciation are you expressing?

I'm sure that you have heard that attitudes are contagious. This certainly is true. Today we have Dave Burgess, teacher and author of *Teach Like a Pirate*, working with our staff. The word *pirate* is an acronym used by Dave, and "p" stands for *passion*. If someone else is excited, it is pretty difficult <u>not</u> to get excited yourself. If someone else is apathetic, you have to work overtime to bring enough energy for both of you. You will have to resist the darkness that the energy vampire tries to draw you into.

It's a fact that we tend to attract and be attracted to like-minded people and people with similar temperaments (Yes, I know I am contradicting the old adage, "Opposites attract."). During my first board meeting as superintendent of Fairfield CSD, I made the questionable move of telling a board member he was "a lightning rod for negativity."

You might not know anything about Fairfield, Iowa, but the average day in this town of 9,500 is a slow news day. The school is news. I hear the comment, "I read about you in the paper," constantly. *The Fairfield Ledger* covers school buildings very well. The lady who writes for the *Ledger* is extremely conscientious and quotes me faithfully. You guessed it: she memorialized the lightning rod quote. Fortunately the board member and I both have a sense of humor. This board member also experienced thanksgetting when I wrote him a note telling him how much I appreciated his comments about the importance of reading during a board meeting. Those comments didn't make the paper, but they were important and I noticed them.

Stephen Covey writes about a concept called *The Emotional Bank* Account. Covey's central point is that we should make deposits in our positive interactions with others, which gives us the needed balance in case we ever need to make a withdrawal. John Maxwell gives one of his *Five Levels of Leadership* to relationships (Level 2). These are wise men. They know that we are created to be in relationship, and the extent to which we have positive relationships determines our success and satisfaction in many instances.

Now consider these ideas in the light of *thanksgetting*. Thanksgetting is <u>transactional</u>. You build up a positive balance with thanksgiving. You feel thankful. You express thanks. You live with an attitude of gratitude, and suddenly your whole view of life changes. You treat people differently. You laugh more. You attract positive people. All of a sudden, you are consistently thanksgetting. It might seem magical, but it's really natural.

Faith is like this. We like to say, "Seeing is believing," but it is much more appropriate to say, "Believing is seeing." If you believe, you see God's hand in everything. You feel joy in your heart. If you don't believe, or if you actively resist belief, you are not going to see what I see. You are not going to experience thanksgiving and thanksgetting like I do. All I can do is treat you like I do believe, hope you get curious about the peace I have, and give the Spirit an opportunity to move in your life. If you have a spirit-filled life, thanksgiving and thanksgetting will become a key part of every day.

Day 23:
Thanksgiving

Today is Thanksgiving, and I have much to be thankful for! I am so thankful for God and for the people and opportunities in my life. Left to my own devices, I have a great propensity to screw things up. I know it's not just me; most of us do. Fortunately, there is help, support, and guidance available to all of us if we seek it. I know I previously wrote about my Big Rocks (Day 2), but this Thanksgiving Day I am going to elaborate a little bit about why I am so thankful for them.

1. Faith—I cannot imagine what life would be like without faith. I was raised in the church by faithful parents, but I don't think my personal faith really developed until I started a family of my own. My family is very thankful to have a church family in Packwood, Iowa. Pastor Harlan "Frosty" Van Voorst and his wife Eunice are remarkable people and great examples of

Christian life and married life. Frosty had a miraculous recovery from cancer that really brought our church together. Frosty was there with his arm around me when my dad died. Frosty pushed me to enroll in the licensed ministry program. I consider Frosty my spiritual father.

Because of the way my faith grew, I did pulpit fill in a number of churches for several years. I loved playing substitute minister, helping congregations out. That led to serving Fairfield First Christian Church as their "full-time/part-time" minister. The official term is *bi-vocational pastor*. Now my family has another church family we really love. My faith determines how I see the world and how I respond to challenges. I cannot comprehend what life without faith would be like.

If humanity were really the end-all, if I were my own highest power, I think I would be discouraged, disappointed, and selfish. I am very thankful for my faith this Thanksgiving Day!

2. Family—I cherish family. I am so blessed with my wife Cindy and sons Jordan and Trey. I am really proud of the people they are and the lives they lead. I take heart in their faith, knowing it will carry them through the challenges.

Most of the older generation of my side of the family is gone. I have enjoyed re-connecting with my mom's sisters, Aunt Glenda and Aunt Sally, throughFacebook. I have three siblings (two brothers and a sister) whom I don't see often, nieces and nephews, and extended family in Wisconsin, too. Many of these relatives I don't have daily contact with, but I know they are family, and I love them.

Today we host the Thanksgiving dinner for Cindy's side of the family. Typically this has been at her parents' house. Cindy has a wonderful family that I have considered my own ever since we married almost 24 years ago. I am thankful this day for the hustle and bustle of family. We don't always have a lot of family around, and it's special when we do. I thank God for my family every day!

3. Work—I am thankful to have meaningful work to do. I often remark that I have no skills or abilities that would allow me to support myself, so I'm fortunate to make a living talking with people. This is basically true, and it makes me the friend of handymen and mechanics, people who do have skills.

I am thankful to have had all of the work experiences I have had, from washing dishes at the Red Rooster, to loading cars in the Hy-Vee drive through in sweltering heat and bitter cold, to teaching everything from seventh grade to college credit English, coaching various sports at different levels, being an activities director, bus driver, principal, superintendent, and pastor.

Through all of these experiences, I know God was equipping me. I appreciate the rigors of restaurant work, so I'm usually a decent tipper. I appreciate service workers of all kinds and am always polite and appreciative. I will admit to getting impatient with customer service representatives on the phone when they have no interest in serving the customer, me! I am not afraid of getting my hands dirty. Honest labor of any kind is noble. For example, everyone in a school plays a critical role: bus driver, custodian, food service worker, maintenance worker, teacher associate, secretary, teacher, and administrator. Every person contributes to a great learning environment for the students we serve.

My work in education and in the ministry has reinforced that God has a plan for me and knows exactly what He's doing. I have had a few professional disappointments. In each case they were short-lived as God opened new doors, and I had opportunities I hadn't even anticipated. We need to be prayerful about work and willing to be stretched. If we are intent on doing God's work in whatever work we do, He will give us great opportunities to serve.

I am thankful this day for faith, family, and work! What are you thankful for?

Day 24:

The Golden Mean

I woke up this morning thinking about the Golden Mean, which basically encourages, "All things in moderation." It is entirely possible that I thought of this because of my Thanksgiving overeating, but I really have internalized a good deal of the Grrek philosophy, drama, and mythology that I have learned and taught through the years. Aristotle usually gets credit for the Golden Mean although the idea has been put forward, developed, and refuted by many others through the years. A Google search of the term quickly returns the Greek letter phi and the number 1.618. Who knew the Golden Mean was a number? Actually, I'm sure math geeks everywhere probably celebrate it and tattoo themselves with it like they do pi. Britannica compares Buddha's middle path between self-indulgence and self-renunciation with the Golden Mean (www.britannica.com). One website blasted the Golden Mean as "a classic example of what's wrong with philosophy" because it doesn't tell you anything (screwplato.wordpress.com). I think the main objection was that "moderate" is hardly quantifiable and varies with the subject. I can understand the objection. Moderate exercise is probably great. Moderate drug use is probably not a good idea.

The concept of the Golden Mean probably appeals to me because it seems to suggest the importance of balance. We know we are going to have highs and lows, peaks and valleys, in life; but if we are balanced, we can stay the course (I think I might have just mixed some metaphors.). As a basketball coach, knowing the team had a long season, I used to try to keep my teams on an even keel, not celebrating the wins too much, being crushed by the defeats too much, or emphasizing any one game too much. I was not a "rah-rah" motivator, and I'm not so sure there weren't times that hurt the team. At least I never accomplished all I wanted to as a coach even though I led competitive, hard-working teams. I should say that I never met all of the goals I had in terms of wins and championships. I have no regrets about the time spent, the relationships with athletes and other coaches, and the lessons I tried to teach kids. As a coach, I gave a lot of encouragement, a lot of correction, a lot of feedback in general, but it was effort/skill-based, not pure emotion. I guess that is usually how I operate today: show up, be consistent, work hard, do things the right way, and try to get better. I am not a charismatic leader. I have read that this is good because those people tend to be a "flash in the pan," impressive for a moment then gone.

I have a self-deprecating description of myself that I share with a co-worker. I call myself a warm bath. You know, kind of nice and comfortable but not that exciting. I think I say this just to get her to retort that that isn't true.

She tells me I'm a visionary leader who gets results. I hate it when people fish for compliments. It's so needy.

The fact is that I really don't know where I stand on this one. It's in that lower right quadrant, Unknown Self, of my Yohari Window (See Day 21). I believe what I heard once: "Too much of anything, even a mother's love, is fatal." I also believe that there are things you'd better be passionate about. As the great John "Cougar" Mellencamp once sang, "You better stand for something, or you're gonna fall for anything." I remember the message given to a church in Revelation 3:16, too: "So, because you are lukewarm—neither hot nor cold—I am about to spit you out of my mouth." I get this. There's nothing worse than a mouthful of lukewarm coffee! The Opportunists in Dante's *Inferno* learned this, too. Because they never committed to anything in life, now they have to eternally chase a banner in Hell while being stung by wasps as they run. Dante describes it a lot better than I do.

Education has sent a lot of mixed messages about this with its emphasis on accountability and standards, as measured by proficiency, defined as 41st percentile on a state test in Iowa. A statistics class I took under duress once taught me the concept of "regression to the mean." That probably explains why we have taught to the middle for so long in education. We hit the most students that way. TAG, IDEA, and RTI (Ask your local educator for definitions.) have helped educators hone in on individual students and their needs. Great teachers aren't on autopilot. They work extremely hard to connect with each student and feel a personal loss when one slips through the cracks. They are committed to continuous improvement. I have had the pleasure of working with a lot of these teachers.

That idea of continuous improvement is important. If we get complacent just because something is good, we become stagnant (School reformers will tell you that is what has happened with Iowa's NAEP, National Assessment of Educational Progress, test scores the last couple of decades.). Jim Collins' book *Good to Great* says it succinctly: "Good is the enemy of great." As a coach, I always tried to get players to buy into continuous improvement. We never stay the same. We are either getting better or getting worse, progressing or regressing. There really isn't a Golden Mean we can find and just stay at.

I do a decent job of keeping perspective and staying on an even keel. I take time to "sharpen the saw" (one of Covey's *7 Habits of Highly Effective People*), primarily through reading, watching TV, dining out, and game playing. The amount of travel I do and number of late nights I have with meetings, basketball games, etc. can be a grind at times. Two recent comments by my wife stick in my mind. As I began one busy week, she asked, "Does anyone else have as many meetings as you do?" I assured her that mine is a "normal" superintendent's existence. At the end of another busy week full of travel, Cindy commented matter-of-factly, "You are going to burn out." I resemble that remark only when I trudge into the room in a hollow-eyed, pre-coffee state (See Day 13).

In an attempt to have a final word and some clarity on the Golden Mean, let me say this: it is healthy to have balance in our lives. BUT we need to have things we are passionate about. I think it is helpful to know what these things are and to know why they are important (See Day 2). Finally, apologies to Aristotle for today's entry.

Day 25:

Creation

I have always greatly admired people's creative work. Artists amaze me. The vision they have and then the ability to make that vision real is astounding. Michelangelo's famous *David*, for example, was carved out of a block of granite that had been worked on and abandoned more than 50 years previously (arthistoryblog.blogspot.com). I think it was Michelangelo who famously answered the question about how he sculpted as follows: "How I sculpt? It is very easy; I get a block of marble and get rid of anything that doesn't look like a lion" (www.themoneyprinciple.co.uk). When I looked for the exact quote, I couldn't find it, but I felt better when this quote appeared on a site discussing "3 Quotes That Will Help You Improve Your Writing" and that person didn't even know who said the quote.

The creative process is amazing, no matter what medium is being used: wood, clay, paint, marble, breath, words, etc.

Consider for a moment how much more amazing the Creation of the World is. God made the world and everything in it out of nothing. God existed in an endless black void. He was when nothing else was. This is hard to imagine. Have you ever entered a space that is truly pitch black and silent? The darkness and silence push in on you oppressively; you can feel it. Even then, though, you can hear your heart beat and feel the ground you stand on. It isn't quite nothingness. God created the heavens and earth, light, water, the sun, the moon, and the stars out of nothing. And it was good. God's creation is amazing and provides the model and inspiration for all great human creative acts that followed.

God gave us seasons in our lives like the seasons we see in nature. Ecclesiastes 3 says this beautifully: "For everything there is a season, and a time for every matter under heaven: a time to be born, and a time to die; a time to plant, and a time to pluck up what is planted; a time to kill, and a time to heal; a time to break down, and a time to build up; a time to weep, and a time to laugh; a time to mourn, and a time to dance; a time to throw stones, and a time to gather stones together; a time to embrace, and a time to refrain from embracing; a time to seek, and a time to lose; a time to keep, and a time to throw away; a time to tear, and a time to sew; a time to keep silence, and a time to speak; a time to love, and a time to hate; a time for war, and a time for peace" (Ecclesiastes 3:1-8, NIV).

Authors throughout history have known this truth and explored it over and over. Jesus used parables about God's natural world—stories about vineyards, crops, and animals—to help people understand God's kingdom. People who understand the beauty and intricacy of creation get a glimpse into the very mind of God.

Can you comprehend the belief that everything in the world was the result of a cosmic accident? Could DNA, the famous double helix that makes each individual who he/she is, be a great randomness? Over time wouldn't the exact same DNA or fingerprints get duplicated by chance in the billions of people in the world? As an accomplished physicist once remarked, "Creation is too beautiful and exquisite for chance."

Different eras have displayed and celebrated man's creative genius. That's how I began today's writing. However, the Enlightenment and today's secular humanism believe mankind is the ultimate authority, capable of all things. I'm sorry; I don't have that much faith in mankind left to its own devices. Mankind as stewards of creation and servants of the Creator, that's another thing!

The old cliché is, "Stop and smell the roses." Take time to do that, or on November 30 in Iowa, to notice the beauty of the patterns in the frost on the windshield or the crispy whiteness of the grass crunching as you walk across it. Nature is good, God is great, and people are crazy (to paraphrase a country song). Enjoy God's creation today and contribute to it any way you can!

Day 26:

School Days

I invite all readers to hearken back to their fond memories of elementary school today. I understand not everyone liked school, and some, like me, have never left school. I know, for me, elementary school still seems like it was a magical time, before the awkwardness of middle school, the organized activities of high school, and the life preparation of college. I had a great elementary school experience at Central School, a neighborhood K-4 building right across the street from my house in Iowa Falls. Now the site is a Fareway store and parking lot, but the big rock we used to climb still stands there with its plaque, commemorating some ancient event or person. For me elementary school was grades kindergarten through four since Iowa Falls sent fifth and sixth graders to the north side of town for "mini-high." If preschool existed then, I didn't know about it. I'm going to share what I remember most clearly from each grade.

K—I attended kindergarten until lunch each day. I remember playing with trucks and blocks and refusing to nap on those blue mats during coerced nap time. What I remember enjoying most about those days was my mom having lunch waiting for me in a metal lunch box when I came home. I usually sat on the kitchen floor and ate with Ellen Ruhde, a little girl a year or so younger than I, whom my mom babysat. It was a very simple, uncomplicated existence I lived.

1st—First grade was very notable because it fueled two important aspects of my being: a love of reading and a competitive nature. I don't know what "SRA" stands for, but it was really kind of a dream for me to have all of these different stories to read in order to be able to progress to a new color after answering questions. All I really remember about first grade was reading everything I could from that SRA box.

2nd—Second grade was the first time I remember writing. I thought a lot of my teacher, Mrs. Steiner, and I turned her into a superhero in a series of "SuperTeach" stories I wrote. I remember her driving around in her Erasermobile, shooting her chalk gun. I also remember getting spanked in second grade (Was there still corporal punishment in 1973?) and unjustly, I thought, getting soap put in my mouth by Mrs. Steiner. My best friend Bart and I called each other "Bart the Fart" and "Art the Fart." If we didn't care, why should anyone else?

3rd—I survived the abuse of second grade to face new trials in third grade. My older siblings had warned me about Ms. Kramer. She was now Mrs. Held. Amazingly enough, someone had married her. She was a stern woman of approximately 95, I thought. Holy cow, did she have a grip, though! Her "Iron Claw," as I thought of it, was something I often felt clamped on the back of my neck and something I emulate today. Mrs. Held was strict, but I know she cared about her students. I am positive I caused her some grief, but I remember her building me up, letting me leave the building to retrieve something she needed from her car during the school day, for example.

4th—I'm going to comment on Central School Principal Mr. Behrends instead of my fourth grade teacher Mrs. Bottke since I'm focusing on my most striking memories. I will never forget Mr. Behrends towering over me, sternly promising, "I'm going to drop on you like a wet blanket!" I didn't even need to understand what he meant to take him seriously and be afraid.

"What led to this scary memory?" you might ask. Let me fill you in. I used to hate drinking milk, especially if it was warm. Central School's milk at lunch was always warm. That's really beside the point, but I'm still trying to rationalize my behavior 37 years or so later.

My good friends Bart Mulford (he of "Bart the Fart" fame) and Terry Schwebke (whom my dad referred to as "Smedford" for some reason) and I decided to smuggle some half-full milk cartons out of the school gymnasium/cafeteria that fateful day. We thought it would be really cool to stomp on them and explode them in the bottom floor boys' bathroom. It was. Really cool. I don't think we anticipated how loud it would be or how much coverage of every surface—walls, mirrors, urinals, etc.—we would get.

Needless to say, we did not get away with it. Some snitch girls heard the echoing blasts, and for all I know, we boys were running around covered in souring milk that afternoon or bragging about our exploits. I don't remember.

I just remember menacing Mr. Behrends standing over me. Ah, the good old days, when a principal could still scare the life out of a kid. Another part of the good old days was that kids who got in trouble at school got in <u>more</u> trouble at home, especially teachers' kids. Can you guess where I was when my large English teacher father got home from work? That's right, cowering in the dark basement, hoping to escape detection. Yeah. That didn't work either.

It's a good thing I'm only writing about K-4 here. I was a good student but not always a good boy. I can't imagine how much more trouble I would have been if we hadn't had truly brutal King of the Mountain and a politically incorrectly named game beginning with *smear* to burn off nervous energy. A lot of things have changed since way back then, many of them for the better. I fondly remember those simple Central School days, though. It was a lot less complicated time, and things were pretty black and white then.

What grade school memories do you hold on to?

K—

1—

2—

3—

4---

Day 27:
The Art of Leadership

I was all set to write on "Fear of Failure" today when, as I was doing my first email run, reassigning emails to the trash or various electronic folders and firing a few of my own off, when I saw today's "Minute with Maxwell." As I shared before, I usually just file this, but there in the subject line were three capital letters: ART. Obviously I felt like it was speaking right to me and I should invest a minute in it. I anticipated something about art that would be similar to my writing on creation (Day 25). I figured I would listen quickly then be done. I was surprised and energized to have the minute be on "the art of leadership."

I don't make any grand claims to leadership though I have had many opportunities to be in what most would consider leadership roles. Some of the most valuable reading and reflection I have done the last 25 years has been on the topic of leadership. In recent years I have thoroughly enjoyed great conversations on the topic of leadership with our older son Jordan. He really gets it. At 23 he is a fine leader because he works hard, treats people right, and seeks continuous growth. That is a great recipe for success. I have always told our sons that whatever their life's work is, if they treat people right and work hard, they will do well.

Maxwell's mission has been leadership development, so when he speaks or writes about leadership, I listen and pay attention. In today's minute he said, "Leadership is an art. There is intuition and subjectivity in leadership." Maxwell notes that people can learn the skills and basics of leadership. If you feel leadership is more science than art, you are probably right that people can achieve some level of effectiveness as a leader from learning how to do various things. If we are talking about what some term "a natural born leader," then I think we are getting beyond learned skills and more into Maxwell's "art of leadership."

In his book *21 Irrefutable Laws of Leadership*, Maxwell presents two laws that deal with the art of leadership, the Law of Intuition and the Law of Timing. Basically, he says that really great leaders find a match between their intuition and their giftedness. They sense opportunity. They hang around others who have figured this out. I know a younger John Maxwell had the opportunity to regularly visit John Wooden, bringing a legal pad of questions with him each time. I can only imagine what a great opportunity and rich conversation that was! Timing is such a huge factor in our lives, too. The thing is, our time is not always God's time or the organization's time. Sometimes we have to have the intuition to accept an opportunity before we think we are really ready; other times we have to have the patience to wait beyond what we think is "our time." I have experienced both of these situations.

Maxwell defines leadership as "influence" and speaks a lot about "adding value." I see the wisdom of these definitions. For me leadership is service. Without exception meaningful leadership opportunities I have had have begun with my willingness to serve. Let's face it: not everyone is willing to put in the extra time or accept the extra responsibility of being a leader when it means being a servant, putting others first. Not everyone is willing to have everyone else's cares/concerns become his/her own. There is a cost.

Many nights I will go home mentally tired from dealing with people and issues all day. Sometimes I feel emotionally drained from trying to achieve results for our students and trying to serve our school staff and my parishioners at church. It is an incredible honor and responsibility to get to serve in leadership roles, though, and I usually bounce back pretty quickly. That's a leadership trait, too: resiliency. It's an interesting paradox that the more I am able to make it not about me, the more I am personally rewarded.

The best leader ever, Jesus Christ, certainly understood the art of leadership. He modeled servanthood and servant leadership. He was the "suffering servant" foretold in Isaiah 53 as well as the King of Kings and Lord of Lords! He humbled Himself and washed His disciples' feet, the work of the lowest servant (See John 13). He even washed Judas' feet, knowing that Judas would betray Him. Jesus did this to try to help the disciples understand how true greatness is achieved. They were worried about seats of honor in Heaven (See Luke 14). He told them the first will be last and the last first and that if they wanted to enter Heaven, they had to have the faith of a child (Luke 18:7).

If you want to understand the art of leadership, by all means read people like John Wooden, John Maxwell, Peter

Drucker, Jack Welch, Margaret Thatcher, and other proven leaders. I also strongly encourage you to study the life of Jesus Christ, my leader and champion!

Day 28:

Good Enough

"Good enough"—what an insidious phrase! The attitude it represents permeates our culture and ensures mediocrity. What does "good enough" indicate? It indicates that we know there is something better, but we are willing to settle for this. Do you really want a good enough marriage? A good enough spiritual life? A good enough relationship with your kids? I don't. Good enough's cousin is, "Let's call it good." "Let's call it good," means, "It's not good, but rather than continuing to persevere, let's quit." What ever happened to living the childhood rhyme I grew up with? "Good, better, best, never let them rest; Till your good is your better, and your better is your best!"

I do not consider myself a perfectionist. If you look at my desk, you will see I am not anal about having everything perfect and under control. However, I have a really hard time accepting that we shouldn't make things as good as we can. Why wouldn't we? Why would we voluntarily subject ourselves to "good enough"? Is it just lack of ambition?

I have a good friend who has bailed me out more than once (not out of jail, for the record). I previously confessed that I am not a handy guy; my friend is a whiz by comparison. He puts the chain back on my chainsaw. He puts stuff together for me. My wife even called him to get my large body off the floor when I passed out from back spasms. He's a worker, a solid guy. One comment he made has stuck with me, though. The comment was three houses, multiple projects, and probably 13 years ago, but I remember it clearly.

Let me set the stage. My buddy and I suspected that the front porch area of my 1900 stucco house needed a new roof. This was an astute observation arrived at just after my friend said, "Artie, I think you might need a new roof here," and then stepped through (fell through) that part of the roof. Happily, there were no injuries, just as there weren't at the next house I owned, when this same buddy was in the elevated bucket of a tractor, running a chainsaw for me.

Amazingly enough, I purchased roofing materials myself, and my friend and I replaced that section of the roof. (I must note that my wife apparently helped on the project. My friend's memory is that she assisted when I was gone running around somewhere.) He was the brains of the operation, and I did as I was told. There were challenges, like six layers of shingles and tiny original nails on the bottom. We persevered. (I just had a flashback to another time on a garage roof of another friend of mine who is also not handy and my falling off his garage into a wagon full of shingles, nails, etc. Fun times!) But I digress. We persevered. To a point. Then the fateful quote came out of

my friend's mouth: "That's good enough. It's just Artie's."
Can you see this statement troubling me? Let's go multiple
choice on the possible reasons why:

A. Art is not that good of a friend, so he really doesn't
   deserve my best effort.

B. I am capable of being a master roofer, but I've always
   felt a few leaks added character to a house.

C. I'm only joking. It's quality craftsmanship, but I like to
   needle my friend.

D. This might not look quite perfect, but it will work. I
   am volunteer labor, and I'm tired. Art doesn't know
   jack crap and couldn't do it himself. This will have to
   do.

I wish "C" were the correct answer, but years of education have taught me the longest multiple choice answer is
usually right, so I think it was "D." I also think this because
the same friend always seems unconcerned by "spare parts"
when he helps me assemble something, and he never looks
at the directions. I really did not intend to make this friend
the showcase for "good enough" because he is awesome, and
he has come to my rescue many times. I just have to laugh at
the situations I get myself into through a lack of handiness.

I think part of our challenge is a lack of patience and
an unwillingness to let things develop. Our culture encourages instant gratification. For example, we pick tomatoes
when they are green instead of letting them ripen and
develop flavor in the U.S. Then we gas them with CO_2 to
turn them some semblance of red. No wonder vine ripened
tomatoes from the garden are better than the "good enough"
we usually eat! Sometimes we need to just keep plugging
away and working hard until the time is right. We should

not consistently settle for good enough. That could be like settling for "or" instead of "and" as the car commercials are famously portraying:

Sweet or Sour

Nuts or Bolts

Large or In Charge

That's some funny stuff there.

Don't settle. John Wooden's Pyramid of Success defines success as "peace of mind which is a direct result of self-satisfaction in knowing you did your best to become the best that you were capable of becoming." The secret is in learning to enjoy the process. The Apostle Paul, shipwrecked, beaten, hungry, imprisoned Paul, said, "I have learned to be content whatever the circumstances" (Philippians 4:11) but not because he had quit striving. Two verses later he famously wrote, "I can do all things through Christ, who strengthens me" (Philippians 4:13). Is it possible for us to learn contentment at the same time we are always striving for improvement? Think about that. I'm going to mull that over, and maybe it will be a topic for another day. Be your best today!

Day 29:

No Stress = Death

It's early December, and a lot of people are feeling stress associated with the holidays. My personal opinion is that a lot of this stress is self-inflicted, but I don't want to sound unsympathetic. Yesterday morning I shared Dr. Zimmerman's Tuesday Tip about alleviating stress with my building staff. They really appreciated his common sense suggestions for reducing stress and setting priorities. We did laugh a little bit about his suggestion to write down everything we were thankful for and then walk around outside alone, saying "Thank you," aloud 1000 times. It was the oddest thing. All day long I couldn't find people I needed at work. I wonder where they were.

The negative health effects of stress are well documented. The website www.webmd.com has an easy-to-read article titled "10 Health Problems Related to Stress That You Can Fix" that I checked out to see if the expected ailments were listed. They were. The top six were heart disease, asthma, obesity, diabetes, headaches, and depression/anxiety. Depression and anxiety were 80% more likely in people with job stress.

I, personally, think the right kind of stress is good and beneficial. I once heard that the only time we don't have stress is when we're dead (I'm not in a hurry to have that kind of stress-free existence because I love my life, but I do know Heaven will be awesome!). I could find articles touting the benefits of stress as quickly as I could those decrying it. Lisa Evans wrote "The Surprising Health Benefits of Stress" for www.entrepreneur.com, for example. The thesis of this article was that brief stress episodes might be beneficial to one's health. People need to assess the kind of stress they are encountering, but short-term stress might actually boost our immune systems. People do need to recuperate after stress, though, which explains why President Obama played 148 rounds of golf his first five years in office. This whole stress management thing is starting to sound a lot like balance. Remember the Golden Mean (Day 24)?

I think stress avoidance to the extreme is unhealthy, just like prolonged stress is. People end up creating new stresses for themselves. Holiday overspending and overeating will have consequences later. If I have a rotten day at work then spend the night in a bar or casino, chances are that tomorrow ain't gonna be a whole lot better! I have taught a couple of books, dystopias (books about future societies gone wrong) that shed light on how our society approaches stress. Bradbury's *Fahrenheit 451* has a scene where a very unhappy housewife overdoses, and a mechanic in grubby coveralls comes out with a portable snake and pumps her stomach. It's no big deal to him; he gets those calls all of the time. She doesn't even remember it happened in the morning. This same woman goes out and drives insanely fast, intentionally hitting animals to bring herself some kind of peace. She's not alone. Others even try to run people down for sport. I am reminded of young people running around in groups playing "Knock 'em out" today. Random targets are picked out on the street and assaulted for kicks. This is happening in our cities today. Huxley's *Brave New World* offers another illustration that hits close to home. Huxley's society does not allow genuine emotion or relationship. There is a lot of genetic engineering, governmental control, and mind control. To handle any stress, people use the drug *soma*. Their mantra is, "A gram is better than a damn." There's a whole lot of self-medicating going on in our society, too. I am not criticizing those who need medication. I just hope we do not have a *Brave New World* where everyone is walking around in a fog (ironic choice of words on this foggy morning). The non-conformist character in Brave New World is John, from the Savage Reservation. He laments at one point, "Nothing costs enough here!" I understand what he is saying. Our human condition is not supposed to be easy. As a side note, John's life is turned into a reality TV show against his will, too (See Day 12).

So much of stress is how we handle it. Charles Swindoll's famous "Attitude" is worth reading (Appendix B). I did not intend to get up at 5:30 this morning. I even asked our auxiliary services director not to call me about the fog since we already had a late start scheduled for professional development. Oops—the neighboring superintendents didn't get the memo, and I had a call and a text by 5:30 A.M. I was only stressed for a minute, and I did not convey any stress to my superintendent colleagues. Instead, I got up, had a bowl of Mini Wheats and a cup of coffee, and started writing. Life is good!

Stress that energizes you and causes you to perform is good. Stress that saps your energy and throws you into a tailspin is bad. As many people have noted, we can't always control what happens to us, but we can learn to control our reactions. We should not be slaves to our circumstances. We should just try to do the right thing and let God handle the results. Much of this book speaks about how to enjoy life and have healthy perspectives. Life is too good and too short to dread it and live stressed out. If you are feeling a lot of ongoing stress, I strongly encourage you to first, seek out the sources of your stress; next, remove what stresses you can by changing contributing actions and habits; and finally, be in prayer about what you cannot change. Actually, prayer is the best place to start. If you are prayerful and thankful, have a sense of humor, and have strong relationships with significant people in your life, stress will not master you.

Let me close with the "Daily Bible Verse" that just popped up on my phone, Romans 8:28: "And we know that for those who love God all things work together for good, for those who are called according to his purpose."

You see? It is all good. Have a great day!

Day 30:
Mental Toughness

Today is one of the rare days when I knew in advance what I wanted to write about: mental toughness. I ran across an article by Amy Morin, a licensed clinical social worker, on www.forbes.com yesterday. It was titled "Mentally Strong People: The 13 Things They Avoid." Then the author had posted a follow up, " 5 Powerful Exercises to Increase Your Mental Strength." It's basketball season, so I was reminded that Jay Bilas had written an article called "Toughness" a few years back for ESPN.com Jay played basketball for Coach K at Duke and then professionally.

I considered myself a mentally tough player when I played basketball, and believe I still exhibit mental toughness. I certainly practice the "5 Powerful Exercises" Amy Morin writes about. Let me share those with you and encourage you to evaluate whether you practice them or whether you should start if you don't:

1. Evaluate Your Core Beliefs—Amy writes, "Whether you're aware of your core beliefs or not, they influence your thoughts, your behavior and emotions." A person who doesn't have clarity on his/her core beliefs is a very confused person, I say! I led this book off with that, Days 1 and 2. Know what you believe then live it.

2. Expend Your Energy Wisely—Amy writes, "Focus on what is only within your control." The basic point is not to waste energy worrying but to focus on being productive.

3. Replace Negative Thoughts with Productive Thoughts—This is an extension of Amy's exercise #2. I have cited Rick Warren's principle of removal and replacement and the importance of positive self-talk (Day 20).

4. Practice Tolerating Discomfort—Amy suggests, "Practice behaving like the person you'd like to become," and she notes that sometimes we need to behave contrary to our emotions. When I wrote about developing talents (Day 17), I mentioned the importance of getting out of our comfort zone. Growth takes toughness and effort.

5. Reflect on Your Progress Daily—Amy notes the importance of quiet reflection. That has been the whole purpose of this book for me (Day 4). I hope you find a way to do this for yourself.

This writer confirmed, for me, that I am practicing the right habits to be mentally tough. This book is not, primarily, a compilation of others' lists, so I won't go through all of the "13 Things to Avoid" or all of Bilas' markers of a tough basketball player. I will cherry pick just a few and encourage you to look up these full articles yourself.

Even if you practice good mental toughness habits, there will continue to be pitfalls to avoid if we want to keep from backsliding. Many of them deal with our relationships with others. I am acutely aware of #5 on Amy's list: mentally strong people can't worry about pleasing others. We are not going to please everyone all of the time. The more complex our jobs or the more people we serve, the truer this is. I try to make informed decisions, involve those who are affected when possible, do the right thing, treat people with dignity, and communicate clearly. None of that ensures everyone's happiness. Amy's #9 thing mentally strong people avoid is, "Resent Other People's Success." This can be tough for people because we fall into the comparison trap. When resources are limited, we want to get ours, whether it's playing time on a team or a percentage of the budget in an organization. Stephen Covey would say this is a scarcity mentality rather than an abundance mentality. Be happy for others' success! Finally, #12 addresses what I see as a huge concern in our society, an entitlement mindset. Amy says mentally strong people avoid feeling the world owes them anything. J.F.K. had it right: "Ask not what your country can do for you but what you can do for your country." I addressed this servant mindset on Day 6.

Jay Bilas notes that fake toughness has no real value. Think of people you know who bluster about how mentally tough they are. They are like the chest thumpers and raise-the-roof players who put on a big show after they make a lay up or taunt an opponent after blocking a shot. Bilas does believe toughness is a skill that can be developed and improved. He identifies a bunch of basketball indicators of mental toughness. I will grab just a few here:

Don't get screened—I'm proud of this part of our son Trey's game. He is not the most physically gifted player on the court any night, but he works hard not to get screened and often causes the screener to cheat and foul him, resulting in an opponent turnover and extra possession for his team. I think we should work to stay out of trouble when we can ("avoid being screened") and should not make it easy for our opponents to score, in basketball and in life. Don't get screened; that's being proactive.

Finish plays—As a player I loved the traditional three-point play and loved contact. My mindset was, "You can't stop me. I am going to get fouled and score the hoop." My best scoring game in high school was against Mt. Pleasant, a current conference rival, at the Iowa State Basketball Tournament in 1984. I scored 53 points (a record at the time), and 17 of those points came from the free throw line (out of 21 attempts). Don't shy away from contact—life is a contact sport—and be sure to FINISH!

Take responsibility for your actions—This particularly applies to mistakes. I wrote about that Day 18. I don't think you need to blow your own horn and take credit when things go well. People notice success. People know who the talented players are. When mistakes are made, though, resist excuse making and finger pointing. If you screw up, acknowledge it, learn from it, and move on.

If you can internalize and operationalize some of these habits for mental toughness, I think you will find life much more satisfying, and you will learn to embrace challenges, which is where we grow. Go get 'em!

How do you show toughness, or what three actions would you say display mental toughness where you work?

1.

2.

3.

Day 31:

Reason

Back when I was beginning this project, I was at a ministers' retreat. One activity was a small group discussion where we shared obstacles we were running up against while others listened and responded. There was a conversation protocol we followed. It was bound to be interesting because we had very different people put together in this intimate little group by the fireplace.

No one was stepping forward to spill his/her guts, so I spoke about a current challenge, which was working with our Teacher Leadership and Compensation (TLC) Committee to try to come up with a new teacher leadership plan. This is significant but messy work that is a key piece of education reform legislation, and the general public has no idea what it's about. I shared this particular challenge with the group because I have a great family life, happy personal life, and strong faith life; what I consider to be challenges usually occur with work demands.

After listening, group members were to say what images came to mind as they were listening. The same young lady I referred to on Day 7 said, "When you were talking, I just saw this great big brain. You said, 'I think,' a lot. I am wondering what you feel." Hmmm. . . that really made me <u>think</u>. I'm not sure how it made me <u>feel</u>. I guess I am fairly analytical, and I'm not overly emotional. I'm not some big, unattached brain, devoid of emotion, though. Her comment was insightful, I thought. Next, a gentleman told me that when I was talking, he felt like I was puking all over. I think he actually said *vomiting*. I know I make people want to puke when I speak sometimes, but I didn't know they felt like I was projectile vomiting all over them. I'm pretty sure this effect was exacerbated by my fast talking, trying to compress ed. reform legislation and collective bargaining into a two-minute window. Another guy reflected that it seemed like maybe I was more comfortable in the messes of life. I replied that my work is messy and complicated at times and that these situations provide great opportunities for leadership. However, I am organized and am a planner, and I love it when things go according to plan!

The conversations the group had really reminded me that people face different challenges in life and that Reason only takes a person so far sometimes. Dante's *Divine Comedy* illustrates this truth well, as Virgil (the great Roman poet) guides Dante through Purgatory. Virgil is the symbol of Reason, but Dante realizes Reason without Faith can only take him so far. Beatrice, the symbol of love and the spirit for Dante, has to take over and guide him because the pagan Virgil can't enter Paradise.

The same is true for our faith journey. Certainly Bible reading and Bible study is essential. We should strive to understand God's Word. Faith is not merely an academic exercise, though. It is ultimately about a relationship with our Savior, Jesus Christ, and about the Spirit moving in our lives.

The Age of Reason, or Enlightenment, as it is called, was a significant era in world history that continues to impact Western thought. It began with the scientific revolution of the 16th and 17th centuries and became associated with French thinkers like Voltaire and the French Revolution of the 18th century (plato.stanford.edu/entries/enlightenment). In America we had Thomas Paine famously writing around the same time, challenging religion and the legitimacy of the Bible (en.wikipedia.org/wiki/The_Age_of_Reason). We can learn a lot from these deep thinkers, and I enjoy studying philosophical essays. We need to learn what Dante learned, though: Reason can only take us so far.

A lot of my professional life has been about developing people's minds; and as a coach, I've helped develop their bodies. My work as a minister has really helped me focus on the heart and the spirit. This is beginning to remind me of Day 24, the Golden Mean. We need both head and heart. We are all interconnected beings with mind, body, and spirit. Reason is not the end-all. I need to remember this because I don't want to be viewed as a big talking brain, sitting like a lump in my chair. If I were, I wouldn't have any arms to grab my coffee! Have a great day everyone!

Day 32:
The Greatest Generation

After staying up too late, watching a movie in which Denzel Washington flew a plane drunk, I wrote today's weight on a calendar that hangs in the kitchen and reminds me that I like to eat and am not too active. Looking back at me was "December 7, Pearl Harbor Day." FDR called it, " a day which will live in infamy," and it is that; but I want to reflect a little bit about what Tom Brokaw called "The Greatest Generation." *The Avengers* is playing on the TV as I type, but the people of The Greatest Generation are the real heroes.

I greatly admire and appreciate military veterans in general. I have an aunt and uncle who served for many years and have worked with and known a large number of brave men and women who have served and been deployed in the Iowa National Guard, which our nation has depended heavily upon. Veterans' willingness to sacrifice and to put their personal and family lives on hold is unbelievable to me.

Those veterans of the Greatest Generation are rapidly disappearing. World War II ended in 1945, sixty-eight years ago, so a young soldier of 20 during the war would be approaching 90 years old. When I think of this generation, my wife's grandpas, Vernon Harms and Gordon Merrill, come to mind. Both are deceased, but I had the pleasure of knowing both as Cindy and I dated and then married.

The traits I think of when I consider The Greatest Generation are a sense of practicality, a determination to enjoy life, a willingness to work, an understanding of commitment, and an air of humility. Both Grandpa Gordon and Grandpa Vernon exhibited these traits very well, and I could add all kinds of other descriptors, too. As I remember Vernon and Gordon, I hope you will think about people you know and admire from this Greatest Generation.

The Greatest Generation probably demonstrated practicality, in part, because they were children of the Great Depression. Figuring out how to "make do" or do more with less is not something many people in our society are very concerned with. Modern consumerism has made personal debt and living beyond one's means the norm. That is not very practical. The debt has to be paid at some point. The Greatest Generation understood this in ways our federal government obviously does not. I'd like to visit with Gordon and Vernon today about what they think about our $17 trillion national debt. Gordon and Vernon were the kind of guys who kept their shop tidy and understood how to fix things. They were common sense, practical guys.

These men enjoyed life, especially their family and friends. Like anyone else, Gordon and Vernon had personal and family health issues to deal with and other challenges that came their way. They loved a family gathering, a ball game, or an evening with friends, though. They appreciated life and the social aspects of life, and I admire that. I was blessed to be a part of many family gatherings at Vernon's house and Gordon's house. Their families continue traditions after their passing. Neither man talked a whole lot about their service, which seems to be another characteristic of the Greatest Generation, but I'm sure that being a POW in a German prison camp for months, eating rats to survive, as Grandpa Vernon did, makes a person appreciate the free life in the United States.

A willingness to work and understanding of commitment are obviously closely related traits, and Vernon and Gordon both clearly exhibited these traits. Vernon worked hard to create a successful business, Harms Oil Company, when he returned from WW II. His success was a source of pride to the family and community. Gordon worked hard, too, as a county worker and minister. His commitment to faith is something I greatly admired during his life. Both of these men of the Greatest Generation were committed to family and work, and they impacted the future generations of their family. I hope I do the same.

A final trait of The Greatest Generation that I will comment on today is humility. I'm not sure anything is more foreign to today's popular culture than humility. We are encouraged at every turn to draw attention to ourselves and seek praise, reward, and notoriety. Grandpa Vernon didn't do that. I never once heard him brag about the business he built or wealth he accrued. He, instead, talked about relationships and friendships he built with customers. Gordon was happiest when he was singing about being "washed in the blood of the Lamb" or when he was relaxing with family in his living room. He wasn't concerned with prestige.

I learned a lot from the example of these two fine men. They were great representatives of The Greatest Generation. I hope modern America never forgets the sacrifice and the example of men and women like them.

Take the time today to pay some attention to people of the Greatest Generation that you encounter.

Day 33:

Expectation

What do you think of when you hear the word *expectation*? Possibly you hear the voice of a parent, coach, or boss, saying, "I have an expectation of. . ." or maybe you think of the phrase "high expectations" and reflect on how your own high expectations have served you well. I'm a fan of high expectations and think everyone should be clear about what he/she expects.

That's not what I am thinking of today when I hear the word *expectation*, though. It is December 8, the second Sunday in the season of Advent. I am thinking about the expectation of the season, as we wait expectantly for the coming of the Christ child.

Why do you think we say, "She's expecting," for a pregnant woman or use the phrase "expectant mother"? I think it's because those women know there is a new life being formed within them. They can feel every kick and movement past a certain point. They are expectant and anxious to see the little part of them that is going to become its own self. By the end of nine months or so, expectant mothers are usually really anxious for the expected blessed event to occur.

Imagine how anxious Elizabeth, Zechariah the priest's wife, must have been to give birth to her son John. Elizabeth had been barren for many years, and to be barren, or infertile, in her time and culture was to be cursed for some sin committed. How expectant must Zechariah and Elizabeth have been to see their son grow into the great trailblazer for the Messiah, John the Baptist, the "voice in the wilderness" (Isaiah 40:3) that would baptize so many in the Jordan River and display the power of the great prophet Elijah?

Consider, too, the expectation of that young Jewish girl Mary, who had been told that she carried the very Son of God! Mary had to be anxious and afraid, but she trusted the divine message she was given, accepted the honor, and "treasured up all these things, pondering them in her heart" (Luke 2:19). When Mary needed reassurance, she undoubtedly found it when she visited her older relative Elizabeth, who was experiencing her own miraculous pregnancy and the expectation that went with it. Elizabeth's baby, who would become John the Baptist, "leapt in her womb" (Luke 1:39) when Elizabeth heard Mary's greeting. Before he was born, John knew the joy and expectation of working for Christ!

If you are a Christian, you are called to expectantly wait for Christ's kingdom. The Bible promises a "new heaven and a new earth" (Revelation 21:1). As we live our lives on earth, waiting expectantly, we do so knowing that Christ has already come. As we move through Advent, waiting for Christmas to get here, we prepare to celebrate what has already happened. Christ is here. He has sent His Spirit to dwell in us until He comes again. Now He sits at God's right hand and intercedes for us. One day He will come back.

The expectation of Advent really is just the joy of knowing the Christmas story. There can be excitement and expectation for the arrival of something new or unknown. There can be adventure in that. It is a sweet expectation, though, anticipating the arrival of something wonderful that we know well. Christians know the Christmas story, and we wait in happy expectation to celebrate Christ's birth.

We know how the story ends. We have the promises of the Author. We don't know every twist, turn, and rough patch we will face along the way. That's a good thing. We would get discouraged if we saw all of the heartache and challenge laid out in front of us. Regardless of our current and future state—through all of the good and bad times we are experiencing and will experience—we know there is a wonderful future in store for the believer. *Expect* it. Live in *expectation*. God bless you!

Day 34:

Communication

It's kind of a travesty that this topic hasn't shown up until Day 34 because communication is about 95% of my work. I had settled on this topic, and right on cue, today's "Minute with Maxwell" popped up with today's word: *articulate*. Maxwell chose the long "a" homonym (are tick you late), not the adjective, and he defined the word as "to make clear." He urged his audience to keep it simple and good naturedly jabbed educators, saying they tend to make the simple complicated while communicators make the complicated simple. He did not excuse himself from the criticism. He related that when he was a young pastor, he took the *Greek New Testament* into the pulpit with him. He wanted the people to see what he knew. "Those farmers didn't care what I knew," he shares today. They wanted to be able to understand and apply things to their lives. In wedding communication to leadership, Maxwell said, "Leaders and communicators cast a vision that shows you how to reach it." That simple sentence wonderfully captures what I see as my life's work, both in school and church.

I was visiting with a Graceland University Ag. Business professor at a ball game Saturday, and he was telling how a nephew of his was studying English and was interested in education leadership but not sure he would want to be an administrator. That made me think of the aforementioned TLC (Teacher Leadership and Compensation) process and the complicated explanation I had given of it (Day 31). It also caused me to reflect on my own path to what I am currently doing. I was an English teacher who had no desire to be a school administrator. What I learned by being a communicator and teacher of effective communication positioned me very well to become an educational leader, though. I shared that point with the college professor. Oral and written communication skills are as important to a school administrator's success as anything else, in my opinion. I would add to that people skills, organization, hard work, a sense of humor, and having a thick skin—all of which I learned through athletics and other activities—as a participant, coach, and activities director.

The importance of communication in our lives cannot be overstated. Even when we know people well, we need to communicate. It is probably true that actions speak louder than words, but people need the encouragement, reinforcement, and accountability of the written and spoken word. I have tried to take a "my word is my bond" approach to life, and I am a firm believer that things become real when we write them. There is power in language! Self-verbalization, teacher clarity, vocabulary programs, classroom discussion, and feedback were all among the top twelve things having the greatest impact on student learning, according to John

Hattie's research (*Visible Learning for Teachers: Maximizing Impact on Learning*, 2012). These things are all clearly related to communication.

I take a pretty basic view of communication, which does not diminish its importance at all. First of all, there needs to be a message, something worthwhile to communicate. Then there needs to be clarity, hopefully followed by some kind of action. The communicator's audience and purpose impact the method of communication and desired action. In Maxwell's example the leader casts the vision and shows people how to reach it. I speak to our school administrators about being keepers of the vision and purveyors of the dream. I speak constantly to my church congregation about the fact that God has a plan, and He keeps His promises. I want them to see this so that they will understand and take the necessary action. It's a similar process in coaching: getting athletes to envision what is necessary for success then getting them to buy in to working toward it. Communication and belief are intertwined.

Communication and leadership hinge on people understanding the message and trusting the person who is sharing it. Speech classes would probably phrase this as "credibility of the speaker." If people understand the vision or goal and acknowledge its value, then they are willing to work and sacrifice for some person, ideal, or cause they trust. We saw this locally as we turned an 85% no vote on a school bond issue into an 84.7% yes vote on a school bond issue three years later. Author Jamie Vollmer's "Four Prerequisites for Progress" were very valuable to me as we worked through this process. I highly recommend his book *Schools Cannot Do It Alone*.

Think about the communication you need to do and how you can communicate clearly and convincingly. What are some concise ideas that underpin your communication? Here are some sample two-word messages that might guide your communication. Think of them as a constant sub text for what you're saying. Try to come up with some of your own:

- Show up.
- Work hard.
- Have fun.
- Be honest.
- Love God.
- Value family.
- Show respect.
- Take care.
- Try again.
- Don't quit.
- Head up.
- Embrace challenge.
- Live life.

It's kind of a fun exercise to pack meaning into two words. Sometimes less is more. Try a few of your own. I want you to communicate with me if I can ever be helpful or if you just want dialogue:

sathofar@gmail.com

Have a great day! Happy communicating!

Day 35:
Leadership Paradoxes

I know some thoughts on leadership have been woven into other days' writing, but today I want to focus on leadership paradoxes. Many people do not understand the mental acuity, the flexibility, and the resiliency involved in being a leader. Being able to tolerate ambiguity, embrace cognitive dissonance, and not be paralyzed by paradoxes—these are leadership characteristics. A leader needs to constantly reframe situations to see opportunity in the midst of difficulty. A leader has to be both focused and flexible. (I was extremely pleased when my outstanding secretary responded with "focused" and "not easily rattled" when I asked her how she would describe me.) A leader needs to have an action bias but also needs to be intuitive about when to stop and reflect. A leader needs to be driven but also needs to be compassionate. With all of these thoughts running through my head, I sought out what others were writing about leadership paradoxes. I came up with a list of ten from Carol

Burbank in her article "Leadership Tensions: Paradoxes that Keep Us Dancing with Our Leadership Story" (leadershipspirit.wordpress.com), "5 Paradoxes of Leadership Development in Asia" from the Center for Creative Leadership and Human Capital Leadership Institute, and three paradoxes from a blog by Simon Sinek. I decided to look for commonality between the three sources and then throw in my own two cents on each grouping, so here we go:

1. "Vision and Openness" (Burbank), "Be close-minded and open-minded" (Sinek), and "To accelerate development, slow down." (Asia)

Certainly vision is key for leadership, so much so that I cringe when I hear or read the phrase "visionary leader" because it has become a buzzword in job postings. I also hear the phrase "laser-like focus" used a lot to describe the kind of tenacity and dedication to the goal that leaders need. I don't disagree with these things; they are Biblical principles. The Apostle Paul writes about "keeping our eyes on the prize" (Philippians 3:14). Jesus Christ certainly knew God's plan and what He had to do. He knew God's timing, too, which people have never been able to understand. Sometimes Jesus said things like, "Don't tell anybody who I am," or "It is not my time." Other times He was more forceful, like when he told Peter, "Get behind me, Satan!" (Matthew 16:23). Jesus knew He needed to get the message out to the Gentiles and lay the foundation for the universal Church, and He knew He couldn't be the earthly king the Jews were wanting. I think about this particular grouping of paradoxes a lot. I am goal-oriented and strive to stay focused on the vision. I am firmly set in my beliefs. Still, I try to be open to possibility because I don't know it all, and I want to be ready to answer the call if God decides to use me in a new way.

2. "For the people but not of the people" (Sinek), "To develop greatness, practice humility" (Asia), "Decisiveness and Listening (Burbank)

Sinek shares a tension that all leaders have probably felt, the separateness that comes with position, coupled with the necessity not to be out of touch. Followers need to know the leader cares, but they don't always want to follow someone they see as exactly like them. Jesus' followers were moved by His compassion and His miraculous power. His own people from Nazareth did not experience this to the same degree as others because they couldn't get past their conception of Jesus as "that carpenter's son." In speakers' circles the joke is that you have to be at least 50 miles from home before you can be considered an expert. Like Jesus said, "A prophet is not without honor except in his own town" (Mark 6:4, Matthew 13:57). Burbank touches on a related theme. Leaders need to be able to make a decision, and they have decision-making authority; but people need to feel heard, and consensus is often important. The Asian authors get right to the heart of it: "To develop greatness, practice humility." This is exactly the message Christ gave His disciples. He reminds them that He is the greatest among them, but he has come to serve (Luke 22:24-30). He tells them the last will be first, and the first will be last (Matthew 19:30, 20:16). He doesn't just <u>tell</u> them either. He <u>shows</u> them by washing their feet, making time for children, spending time with society's outcasts, bringing healing and compassion, and humbling Himself on the cross. There are countless books written about servant leadership, but if you are really interested in understanding what that means, study the life of Jesus Christ, who came to serve, not to be served.

3. "To excel at the task, harness relationships." (Asia), "Planning and people" (Burbank), and "Delegate responsibility but maintain control" (Sinek).

As I read these paradoxes, I think of the phrase "loose-tight leadership," which is how the Iowa Department of Education describes its relationship with local school districts in a state that has traditionally valued local control. Local boards and administrators tend to get their feathers ruffled at state mandates, especially unfunded or underfunded mandates, of which there have been a few through the years. The DE sets a vision for state schools and often has knowledge and expertise exceeding that of the people responsible for enacting the vision. The challenge is supporting and pushing local districts at the same time. This is a macro version of what happens on a micro level with leaders every day. Whether it's the DE trying to ensure a commitment to continuous improvement by Iowa schools, a superintendent trying to foster a vision and spur various stakeholders to contribute, a teacher trying to get a class to buy in to the importance of learning a concept, or a principal providing feedback to help a teacher improve professional practice, all of these involve tasks and relationships.

The old cliché is that students don't care how much teachers know until they know they care. I don't think it is any different for any other leader. Motivation matters. Self-serving people do not inspire commitment in others. The best planner in the world can't carry out all of the work himself/herself. It is about both planning and people, as Burbank stated. Sinek's "delegate responsibility but maintain control" seems to have a little more command and control flavor to it, but I think this is responsible leadership. People in the organization want to believe and need to know that their leaders have things under control.

Two related phrases that I espouse are "defined autonomy" and "trust but verify." Defined autonomy isn't that different from the DE's "loose-tight" concept. Basically, with defined autonomy, the leader sets the tone, saying, "This is where we're going, but you have the freedom to use your skills and creativity to decide how we're getting there." The Iowa Core curriculum standards provide an example: teachers are expected to align instruction with the standards, but administrators usually do not want to stifle creativity by telling teachers exactly what and how to teach. "Trust but verify," is an old Ronald Reagan Cold War reminder. Arms reductions treaties are great, but let's make sure Russia is really decommissioning nukes as promised. The international community has been duped by rogue nations like North Korea and Iran, who asked the world to trust them without allowing proper verification. Maybe Reagan wasn't so far off with his "Axis of Evil" comments, but I digress.

Once again, these concepts are very Biblical. The greatest commandments are, "Love the Lord your God with all your heart, mind, soul, and strength," and "Love your neighbor as yourself" (Matthew 22:37-39). These are visionary statements about how to live. How we accomplish these tasks is totally up to us. I can think of a lot of ways to love God and love our neighbors. I'll close today with an extension of yesterday's two-word activity and encourage you to make your own list.

- Give thanks.
- Smile freely.
- Open doors.
- Offer prayer.
- Give hugs.
- Extend assistance.

- Forgive unconditionally.
- Praise God.
- Give generously.
- Love life.

Interesting how leadership turned into love and how paradoxes melted away into two important tasks! God bless you!

Day 36:

Peace

I was sitting here after an early morning meeting, trying to think of what to spend one of the last few days of writing on. Behind my desk on the wall, I read, "You will keep in perfect peace him whose mind is steadfast, because he trusts in you" (Isaiah 26:3). I have always thought the "peace that passes understanding" is one of the Bible's greatest promises. Philippians 4:7 actually reads something like this, depending on the translation: "And the peace of God, which transcends all understanding, will guard your hearts and minds in Christ Jesus." That's awesome! We can experience God's peace, and it will guard our hearts and minds (Day 31). Is there anything this world cries out for more than peace?

Jill Jackson Miller and Sy Miller famously put out that call in their 1955 song "Let There Be Peace on Earth." I want to draw your attention to the first line of that song, and if you have the tune in your head, feel free to sing it: "Let there be peace on earth, and let it begin with me." Are you a starry-eyed optimist? Do you believe one person can make a difference? You'd better be. The world is a collection of ones. I'm sure you have heard the starfish story, about the person walking the beach and throwing starfish back in the ocean after they had washed up on the beach. When confronted with the enormity of the task and the futility of continuing, being told that he couldn't possibly make a difference, he replied, with starfish in hand, "It makes a difference to this one." As a side note, that's an awfully good illustration of what teaching is like sometimes.

That's how it is with peace. It makes a difference if you are at peace. I guarantee you that if you have the peace that passes human understanding in your heart, you are going to positively impact others. Your peace will lead you to be more patient with others. It will help you "keep your head when all about you are losing theirs and blaming it on you" (See Appendix C for Rudyard Kipling's poem "If"). It will make you much more likely to exhibit the fruit of the spirit: love, joy, peace, patience, kindness, goodness, faithfulness, gentleness, and self-control (Galatians 5:22-23).

I would go so far as to say that if we are at peace with the world and ourselves, nothing else matters. For me there is a qualifier that peace comes from knowing I am a child of God, saved through Jesus Christ. If we are at peace, then our circumstances do not have the power to destroy us. The external does not rule the internal.

Think of it this way. Have you seen those luxury car commercials where there is noise, confusion, and hubbub all around; but when you get in the car and close the door, you are transported into a world of comfort, quiet, and luxury?

In case luxury automobiles aren't part of your existence, have you ever been buttoned up nice and warm and safe inside when a blizzard raged just outside your window? That's peace. I'm sure you have seen the radar graphics of swirling hurricanes with "the eye of the storm" clear at the center. I have heard there is a preternatural calm at the eye of the storm. You probably have sat outside on a warm, sticky summer night (especially if you live in Iowa) when everything was still just before all heck broke loose with Mother Nature. That's the "calm before the storm." I'm not suggesting your peace has to give way to chaos though we all have little eruptions in our lives. I'm just trying to get some images in our minds about how peace can exist in a tumultuous world.

One more image I remember from some reading I did during my ministry studies was that we are in permanent white water. Think rubber raft being tossed around a roiling Colorado River. When you're in white water, you'd better be sure you have your life jacket. Your life jacket is your core beliefs. That is how you can enjoy the ride with some semblance of peace.

If this book does nothing else than illuminate my core beliefs, to anyone else's benefit, I will feel it has been a huge success. I am so thankful for the peace that comes from knowing God and living my core beliefs!

"Peace I leave with you; my peace I give you. I do not give to you as the world gives. Do not let your hearts be troubled and do not be afraid" (Jesus' words in John 14:27).

Day 37:

Be a Magnet

I was tempted to write about being a *magnate*, but I'm not really qualified for that, and that's not really a thought that is consistent with the rest of the book. Thank you to my curriculum director, though, who gave me the idea late in the afternoon when she said something like, "People are just drawn to you, aren't they?" Don't worry; my head is not exploding. This comment was in response to an impromptu meeting I had with an employee who stopped in for a little career counseling as she considered professional growth. I was glad to get the idea. I have been writing in the morning but started today with a splitting headache that chose to hang around, so I had not written.

I do get a fair number of requests for advice or input, people dropping in, invitations to speak or serve, etc. It is a good thing to attract requests and to know that you can help others. I'm pretty sure anyone reading this book can be a magnet for that type of thing, too, once people know you're willing. They probably won't ask in the first place, though, unless they know you care about people and have a servant's heart. If you do attain that kind of reputation, requests will come. One of my favorite requests is when people ask me if I will pray for them or a loved one or a particular situation. Sometimes this comes directly through my church affiliation, as it did tonight with a prayer chain request. Often it is more incidental. Someone knows I am a Christian and believes in the power of prayer—or figures it couldn't hurt anything—whatever the case may be, and he/she asks if I will pray. I'm happy to do that. I know, "There is power in a righteous person's prayer" (James 5:16). I really love it when someone tells me he is praying for me! Complete strangers have come up to me in the grocery store and said things like, "You're doing a great job. I'm praying for you!" and "I'm so glad Fairfield has a Christian superintendent." That's powerful stuff. That will float your boat for a while.

I was just reading a book called *Leadership Axioms* by Bill Hybels last night, and he was writing about the importance of "hiring tens." Attracting good leaders is so important, but we can't be magnets for them if we aren't developing ourselves as leaders. If you're a "5" on the leadership scale, you aren't going to attract an "8" or "9" to follow you. I feel very good about the leaders I have been able to help hire as well as those who were there before me. They push me to get better and make our organization strong. They are magnets for other great staff members, too. John Maxwell writes about this leadership magnetism in *The Five Levels of Leadership*, a book I highly recommend, as well.

It wouldn't be a complete entry on being a magnet if I didn't write something about repelling as well as attracting.

Now I really do not want to encourage you to be repugnant to others, but there are certain people and behaviors that I hope you repel, to some extent, because they are incompatible with your values and contrary to your nature. For example, some of my first words to the district's assembled teaching staff when I was a new superintendent were, "We're probably going to get along great unless you are lazy, whiny, or dishonest." I just don't have time for those things. As a coach or sports fan, I don't have a lot of time for players who are soft or those who insist on being drama queens. As a Christian, I get impatient with hypocrisy even though I recognize I can act like a Pharisee myself sometimes. As a parent, I don't respect other adults who refuse to parent their kids. I am who I am, and I don't tend to attract the kinds of things I just mentioned, and I spend as little time as possible around them.

I don't have to tell you how influential peer groups are. You know if you lie down with the pigs, you're going to get dirty. If you spend every afternoon "catching up" with the town gossip, you are destined to *become* the town gossip. Why do we worry about the people our kids hang with when they're growing up or comment on some other person's bad habit yet not look in the mirror and consider what <u>we</u> are magnets for? That's what the old poem "The Man in the Glass" (See Appendix D.) encouraged me to do when I read it as a young hoops player.

Be a magnet. Attract the right people and things and repel the wrong people and things. I understand that sounds a little judgmental, and I know Jesus hung out with the lepers, tax collectors, prostitutes, and sinners of His day. You can show kindness or give assistance to anyone. Just be on your guard.

Maybe you could take a minute and think about what you are a magnet for. I encourage you to embrace the opportunity to be a magnet for the right things and people!

Day 38:
Reflection

Reflection—I'm writing about two meanings of this word today because that's what English teachers do. It makes us feel smart. If you picked up this book and have continued to read through Day 38, then you probably appreciate the value of personal reflection. Honest self-examination is a critical component of any kind of personal growth. Without it we become stagnant. Stagnant is not good. Picture a potentially beautiful, sparkling farm pond (We have them all over Iowa!). Now see that pond covered in thick, slimy neon green algae. That's stagnant. It's just a fact; we either work at getting better, or we don't get better. It's another fact that we can work like crazy, unproductively, and not make the gains we should. Our work has to be focused and grounded in a vision. Enter reflection.

The other kind of reflection is what you present to others. What story does your life tell? Do you walk the talk? Are you providing authentic leadership? Obviously I believe our lives should be a reflection of our values. A number of Bible verses refer to refining fire; silver is refined when the refiner can see his reflection in it. I think about "The Bean," one of those great Chicago landmarks. I know it's not real silver, but it is very striking to walk up to this huge silver kidney-bean-shaped sculpture and see the world around it reflected in living color. I wonder what kind of reflection we are giving to the world.

How have we responded when we have gone through the fire? Have we reflected love and faith and leadership? There's a song that has as its refrain, "And they'll know we are Christians by our love, by our love. Yes, they'll know we are Christians by our love" ("They'll Know we are Christians by our Love," Peter Scholtes, 2007). Are we reflecting the love of Christ in our lives as his followers? You know, Christians sometimes give Christianity a bad rap by being judgmental, legalistic, and exclusive. There's a distinct difference between religion and faith. Religion too often is dogma, separation, and man-made hierarchies. Faith is a personal relationship with our Maker, played out within our lives and with a community of believers. Which one of these, religion or faith, do you want to reflect? Knowing your Bible isn't enough. The Pharisees and Sadducees knew their Bible (Torah) and rejected Christ and put Him to death. Don't kill Christ all over again. Let Him live in your life and be reflected in your walk.

Christianity aside, whatever one's faith, one's life can reflect sound values, good citizenship, and concern for others. The world will be a better place if it does, and we can impact the world one life at a time. Have a great day, and let your life shine!

Day 39:

Believe

I'm getting an early start on today's writing. It's about 12:20 A.M. at a SpringHill Suites in West Des Moines. The unhappy occasion (for Iowa Hawkeye fans) is an 85-82 loss to the in-state rivals, the Iowa State Cyclones, in Ames tonight. How did those pesky 16th rated Cyclones come away with a win when they were outrebounded by fourteen and only led for 2:50 of the forty-minute game? Easy— they believed in what Cyclone fans sometimes obnoxiously proclaim as Hilton Magic. The 'Clones are very tough at home. The Hawkeyes, who led almost all of the game, evidently didn't believe they could score down the stretch. They didn't have a field goal the last 2:04 of the game, and they were 1-6 from the free throw line the last four minutes. Confidence is a funny thing. It comes and goes, especially for young people in intense situations. A player might make a huge three-pointer one possession then make a horrible turnover or miss a key free throw the next. Isn't that just like life?

There is a Biblical figure who is emblematic of this struggle to believe that we all have sometimes. Mark 9:14-29 is an account of a man whose son was demon possessed. The man addressed Jesus, informing Him that His disciples had been unable to drive out the spirit. The father asked Jesus to help if He could. Can you imagine Jesus' reaction to that? Was He amused? Annoyed? Jesus replied, "If you can? Everything is possible for one who believes" (23). Jesus was speaking to His disciples here, too. The father's reply is what makes him the poster boy for us doubters: "I do believe; help me overcome my unbelief" (24). You know how the story ends. Jesus rebuked the spirit and the boy was healed. We all have those moments when our belief is tested. I once read that Mother Teresa suffered from depression for decades and left behind writings that showed she suffered very deep crises of faith off and on. Surrounded by the squalor, suffering, and disease of Calcutta, I can understand how this would happen. She just kept helping others, though, and I bet she uttered a prayer like the father's more than once.

I have written about knowing that our Redeemer lives (Day 5), the voices we listen to (Day 20), and peace that comes from knowing God (Day 36). These are all important elements of and byproducts of our belief. Our belief gets cemented in our lives as we experience various trials and blessings. That is typically how it works with achievements, too, athletic or otherwise. We put in the time and work, we have some success, we gain confidence in our ability to perform, and this confidence engenders more success. If God is in all of these efforts, there can be miraculous results. This is more or less how a player becomes a major college athlete who makes over 80% of his free throws. No one is immune to doubt or distraction, though. Sometimes we visualize negative things happening—we listen to the wrong voice, that one of nagging doubt—then what was feared occurs, a self-fulfilling prophecy! That happens at the free throw line. Looking into a red pulsating sea of loud, obnoxious Cyclone fans could be a little distracting. We get distracted in our lives, too, sometimes.

It's one of the great ironies of life that by the time we have things somewhat figured out, we no longer have the energy to capitalize. (I understand this is a sweeping statement and on the pessimistic side.) Knowing what I know now, I'd be a heck of a basketball player if I weren't middle aged and overweight, gimping around on crappy knees. There is a little window of time when we have some of the best of both. That's why crafty old men can sometimes beat athletic young guys at rec league ball. I believe now that the free throw is a very easy shot. I know how to relax, focus, and enjoy the moment. I would be visualizing success instead of failure. I believe I could have carried the Hawks to victory at the free throw line. It's too late, though. There's no turning back the clock on my hoops career, and I wasn't a Division 1 athlete anyway.

It's never too late to believe in God, though! Read the parable of the workers (Matthew 20:1-16). Those showing up in the eleventh hour got a full day's wage. How about the thief on the cross? He waited until the very end of his life but was assured he would see Jesus in Paradise that day (Luke 23:32-43). I don't recommend waiting, but it's never too late to believe. We have a generous and forgiving God who <u>wants</u> us to be saved. Just <u>believe</u>. Accept the gift. I promise you your life will never be the same again.

You won't see the world and its challenges the same way anymore. You will trust that God can use you in ways you can't even imagine. You will believe that if He brings you to it, He will bring you through it. It's okay if you're not sure. Just try to trust God. Say that prayer the father said: "I do believe; help me to overcome my unbelief."

"Blessed be the God and Father of our Lord Jesus Christ! According to His great mercy, He has caused us to be born again to a living hope through the resurrection of Jesus Christ from the dead, to an inheritance that is imperishable, undefiled, and unfading, kept in heaven for you, who by God's power are being guarded through faith for a salvation ready to be revealed in the last time" (1 Peter 1:3-5).

Day 40:

Home

Dorothy had it right when she said, "There's no place like home." I'm not a *Wizard of Oz* expert, but I think that repeated sentence had some magical power to get her back to Kansas. Whether you're been through a whirlwind, on the road, or just through a long day at the office, I hope you have a "home sweet home" to go to and that "home is where the heart is" for you. I am extremely thankful to have the home base and the family I do to come home to. I am truly blessed. In this introductory paragraph I have thrown out several of the time worn platitudes about home Now let me have some English teacher fun with words as I work through a *home* vocabulary list.

- *home sick/homesick*—What a difference a space makes! Our son Trey is home sick today. Last week he finished finals and did well. Last night he helped his college basketball team to a win and a 10-2 record heading into break. This morning (early) we were wakened by unpleasant sounds as the stomach flu made an appearance. Sick is no fun, but if you must be sick, home sick is the way to go. *Homesick* is entirely different, and homesickness afflicts some much more strongly than others. When my wife Cindy was heading to college to play basketball, she chose a scholarship from the University of Northern Iowa, just a half hour from home, instead of one from DePaul University in Chicago. She knew she was a homebody (bonus *home* word).

- *home bound/homebound*—Part two of the space words! We like to be on the go, and we enjoy seeing new places, but there is always a comfort in being home bound. I think it was Simon and Garfunkel who sang a great song, "Homeward Bound"; you should check that out. Even at the end of a long workday, it's just nice to be bound for home then pull into the driveway. *Home bound* is good. *Homebound* is sometimes heart-wrenching. For some home becomes a kind of prison. It's great to get home when you've been away, but what if you can never get out? What if you can never get out, and the world never comes in? It is really important to keep the homebound in prayer, take them out if possible, send them cards, visit them, offer them communion, etc. People are living longer, but that's not always easy. For many people the only thing worse than being homebound is no longer being able to be in their own home. I've seen this with my mother and many church members. It is a Biblical principle to care for the infirm and aged. I hope we take that to heart.

- *Home cooking*—This is one of my personal favorites. My dad was a great cook, and my mom was pretty good, too. Cindy's mom is an unbelievable "Food Network" type cook, and her dad works a grill with the best of them. Cindy and I love to eat, and you can't beat home cooking! Besides the obvious sensual appeals—the smells, sights, textures, and tastes of great home cooked food—there are other benefits. Just like coffee time (Day 13), food brings people together. It's <u>communal</u>. Jesus didn't institute the Lord's Supper by accident. He broke bread with the disciples. He ate and drank (See Matthew 26, Mark 14). After His resurrection Jesus cooked fish over a fire and served His disciples breakfast (John 21). There is power in coming together over a meal, and the best option is a home cooked meal with family and/or friends. Don't forget to give thanks when you have this opportunity. It is a blessing.

- *Homework*—I just lost any teenage readers I had on Day 40. I don't think they were the target audience anyway. We have all probably felt the pain of homework sometime. There comes a point when it seems less of a fruitless activity or exercise in busywork and more of a growth opportunity. When you begin feeling that way, you have probably become what we call a "lifelong learner." Homework for a lifelong learner is less likely to be something someone else assigned and more likely to be something sought by you for personal growth. Anyone with much work experience or anyone seeking work sees the value in "doing your homework," in other words, preparing for that meeting, presentation, or interview. Whenever possible we should try to prepare for what we might face even when we don't know exactly what it will be. One thing we can be sure of is that we will face judgment one day. Do your homework. Know your Bible. Get to know your Judge before that day.

- *Homecoming*—Does this word conjure up the excitement of high school dress up days, float building, dances, and football games? Homecoming is a fond memory for many. For others it wasn't that big of a deal. For some it might even mark a time of disappointment: being hurt for the big game, not having a date for the dance, etc. Life is full of these highs and lows. Sometimes people have a homecoming of sorts when they move back to town to live and work or raise a family. Some people never come back. Some people never leave in the first place. *Homecoming* can have a lot of connotations. I firmly believe we are just visitors on this earth. We are citizens of Heaven (Philippians 1:27, 3:20). We have a spark of the divine in us because we were created in God's image (Genesis 1:27). How we live our life on this earth and what we believe during our fleeting time here has eternal consequences! My prayer for all of us is that we have a heavenly homecoming where our God says to us, "Well done, good and faithful servant" (Matthew 25: 21, 23). I really believe that's the whole point of this life, preparation for the next life. That is a homecoming I look forward to!

I want to thank anyone who read this book for going on this little journey with me, and I encourage you to reflect on some of the same things I just have. Life is good, full of so many opportunities for us. I wish you all reflection and peace in the midst of your busy lives!

Appendix A

A Poison Tree

I was angry with my friend:
I told my wrath, my wrath did end.
I was angry with my foe:
I told it not, my wrath did grow.

And I watered it in fears,
Night and morning with my tears;
And I sunned it with smiles,
And with soft deceitful wiles.

And it grew both day and night,
Till it bore an apple bright.
And my foe beheld it shine.
And he knew that it was mine,

And into my garden stole
When the night had veiled the pole;
In the morning glad I see
My foe outstretched beneath the tree.

William Blake

Appendix B

ATTITUDE
by
Charles Swindoll

"The longer I live, the more I realize the impact of attitude on life. Attitude, to me, is more important than facts. It is more important than the past, than education, than money, than circumstances, than failures, than successes, than what other people think, say or do. It is more important than appearance, giftedness or skill. It will make or break a company... a church... a home. The remarkable thing is we have a choice every day regarding the attitude we embrace for that day. We cannot change our past... we cannot change the fact that people will act in a certain way. We cannot change the inevitable. The only thing we can do is play the one string we have, and that is our attitude... I am convinced that life is 10% what happens to me and 90% how I react to it.

And so it is with you... we are in charge of our Attitudes"

Appendix C

"If" by Rudyard Kipling

IF you can keep your head when all about you
Are losing theirs and blaming it on you,
If you can trust yourself when all men doubt you,
But make allowance for their doubting too;
If you can wait and not be tired by waiting,
Or being lied about, don't deal in lies,
Or being hated, don't give way to hating,
And yet don't look too good, nor talk too wise:

If you can dream - and not make dreams your master;
If you can think - and not make thoughts your aim;
If you can meet with Triumph and Disaster
And treat those two impostors just the same;
If you can bear to hear the truth you've spoken
Twisted by knaves to make a trap for fools,
Or watch the things you gave your life to, broken,
And stoop and build 'em up with worn-out tools:

If you can make one heap of all your winnings
And risk it on one turn of pitch-and-toss,
And lose, and start again at your beginnings
And never breathe a word about your loss;
If you can force your heart and nerve and sinew
To serve your turn long after they are gone,
And so hold on when there is nothing in you
Except the Will which says to them: 'Hold on!'

If you can talk with crowds and keep your virtue,
Or walk with Kings - nor lose the common touch,
If neither foes nor loving friends can hurt you,
If all men count with you, but none too much;
If you can fill the unforgiving minute
With sixty seconds' worth of distance run,
Yours is the Earth and everything that's in it,
And - which is more - you'll be a Man, my son!

Appendix D

The Man in the Glass
by Dale Wimbrow, (c) 1934
1895-1954

When you get what you want in your struggle for self,
And the world makes you King for a day,
Just go to the mirror and look at yourself,
And see what that man has to say.
For it isn't your Father, or Mother, or Wife,
Whose judgment upon you must pass.
The fellow whose verdict counts most in your life
Is the man staring back from the glass.

You may be like Jack Horner and "chisel" a plum,
And think you're a wonderful guy,
But the man in the glass says you're only a bum
If you can't look him straight in the eye.
He's the fellow to please, never mind all the rest,
For he's with you clear up to the end,

And you've passed your most dangerous, difficult test
If the man in the glass is your friend.
You may get what you want down the pathway of
years,
And get pats on the back as you pass,
But your final reward will be heartaches and tears
If you've cheated the guy in the glass.

Afterword

Writing this book has been a great experience. There certainly were days when I did not feel "inspired" to write, but I have heard many authors emphasize the discipline of writing. Writers write; they do not wait for inspiration. I know that my life is nothing remarkable, but I do feel remarkably blessed. More than anything else, I want people to know the joy I feel in faith, family, and work. If the reader doesn't feel his/her own peace and joy, my hope is that my suggestion to be reflective and spiritual can help bring those things. Thank you so much for taking the time to read the book. Best wishes to you for a fulfilling and purpose-filled life! Let me leave you with an old poem I really like that never fails to provide the attitude check I need.

Wreckers or Builders?

I watched them tearing a building down,
A gang of men in a busy town.
With a ho-heave-ho and lusty yell,
They swung a beam and a sidewall fell.
I asked the foreman, "Are these men skilled,
As the men you'd hire if you had to build?"
He gave me a laugh and said, "No indeed!
Just common labor is all I need.
I can easily wreck in a day or two
What builders have taken a year to do."
And I tho't to myself as I went my way,
Which of these two roles have I tried to play?
Am I a builder who works with care,
Measuring life by the rule and square?
Am I shaping my deeds by a well-made plan,
Patiently doing the best I can?
Or am I a wrecker who walks the town,
Content with the labor of tearing down?

Author Unknown

About the Author

Art Sathoff grew up in small town Iowa valuing faith, family, and hard work. These remain core values of the Sathoffs to this day. Art graduated from Iowa Falls High School in 1984 and went on to study English Education and play basketball at Wartburg College in Waverly, Iowa, where he was the Outstanding Senior English Graduate and Outstanding Senior Male Student Athlete in 1988. He earned an M.A. in English Literature at the University of Northern Iowa in 1993 and principal's certification, followed by an Ed.S. degree from Drake University in 2004. In 2009 he finished the licensed minister's program through the Christian Church of the Upper Midwest. Currently he serves as superintendent for Fairfield Community School District and pastor at Fairfield First Christian Church.

He lives in Fairfield with his wife of 24 years, Cindy. Cindy and Art have two sons: Jordan, who works in the investment field, and Trey, who is in college. Art has been employed in public education in a variety of roles for 26 years.

www.ingramcontent.com/pod-product-compliance
Lightning Source LLC
Chambersburg PA
CBHW030831090426
42737CB00009B/963